D1327270

This is number 40 of

125 specially prepared and signed

copies of *Prime Fathers*

in honor of

The Western American Literature Association

Frederick Manfred

PRIME FATHERS

BOOKS BY FREDERICK MANFRED

The Golden Bowl	1944
Boy Almighty	1945
This Is the Year	1947
The Chokecherry Tree	1948
The Primitive	1949
The Brother	1950
The Giant	1951
Lord Grizzly	1954
Morning Red	1956
Riders of Judgment	1957
Conquering Horse	1959
Arrow Love (stories)	1961
Wanderlust*	1962
Scarlet Plume	1964
The Secret Place**	1965
Winter Count (poems)	1966
King of Spades	1966
Apples of Paradise (stories)	1968
Eden Prairie	1968
Conversations***	1974
Milk of Wolves	1976
The Manly-Hearted Woman	1976
Green Earth	1977
The Wind Blows Free (reminiscence)	1979
Sons of Adam	1980

* A revised version of a trilogy that was originally published in separate volumes as *The Primitive, The Brother,* and *The Giant.*

** Originally published in hardback as *The Man Who Looked like the Prince of Wales.*

*** Moderated by John R. Milton.

Frederick Manfred wrote under the pen name of Feike Feikema from 1944 through 1951.

Prime Fathers

Frederick Manfred

Howe Brothers

SALT LAKE CITY

1988

"Wanted, More Ornery Cusses" appeared originally
in the CHICAGO TRIBUNE;

Sinclair Lewis: A Portrait appeared originally
in THE AMERICAN SCHOLAR;

Hubert Horatio Humphrey: A Memoir appeared originally
in MINNESOTA HISTORY;

Ninety Is Enough: Portrait of My Father appeared originally
in THE IOWA REVIEW;

The Artist as the True Child of God appeared originally
in SOUTH DAKOTA REVIEW;

Report from Minnesota: Introducing Hubert H. Humphrey
appeared originally in THE NEW REPUBLIC; and

West of the Mississippi: An Interview with Frederick Manfred
appeared originally in
CRITIQUE: STUDIES IN MODERN FICTION

published by

Howe Brothers — Salt Lake City, Utah

Manufactured in the United States of America

LIBRARY OF CONGRESS CATALOGING-IN-PUBLICATION DATA

Manfred, Frederick Feikema, 1912–
    Prime fathers.
    1. Manfred, Frederick Feikema, 1912–   . 2. Authors,
American — 20th century — Biography. 3. Humphrey, Hubert H.
(Hubert Horatio), 1911–1978. 4. Lewis, Sinclair, 1885–
1951. 5. Minnesota — Biography. I. Title.
PS3525.A52233Z476   1988   813'.54 [B]   86-27847
ISBN 0-935704-36-1
ISBN 0-935704-37-X (pbk.)

Contents

Foreword by Mick Mc A llister   ix

"Wanted: More Ornery Cusses"   1

PRIME FATHERS

1   Hubert Horatio Humphrey   5

2   Ninety Is Enough: Portrait of My Father   35

3   Sinclair Lewis: A Portrait   66

4   The Artist as the True Child of God   97

SCRAP BOOK

5   Report from Minnesota: Introducing
    Hubert H. Humphrey   117

6   On Being a Western American Writer   122

7   In Memoriam Address: Sinclair Lewis, 1885–1951   139

8   West of the Mississippi:
    An Interview with Frederick Manfred   151

Foreword

Back when Frederick Manfred and I were still a bit stiff-legged and high-tailed around each other, I once mentioned that I thought the ending of his novel *Conquering Horse* was a wonderful twisting into American myth of *Oedipus at Colonus.* "*Oedipus at Colonus,*" he said innocently. "Is that a Sophocles play?" Ever the American and Americanist, Manfred dramatizes his role as "a Mark Twain man," untrained original, rooted in the English of Chaucer. When Manfred speaks of his literary roots, in "The Artist as the True Child of God," "On Being a Western American Writer," and "West of the Mississippi," he neglects to mention the Greek dramatists, but they are there in the crowded room of literary ancestors, Sophocles at least one unmentioned "prime father."

In what sense are the fathers celebrated here "prime"? It's tempting, knowing Frederick Manfred's relationship to the American language, to assume he means "primal" but chooses to drop the affected European syllable. In fact, "prime" means "first" and these are Manfred's First Fathers, but "prime" puts a twist of solidity to the commonplace. These are prime fathers like good meat, not so much masters as men he has, sometimes uneasily, been the son of. We choose our masters, and they choose us, but fathers and sons simply have each other. They are shaped by each other,

ix

and when their relationship works best, they grow away from each other like two trees that cannot occupy the same place. Fathers and sons are bound by love, which forgives rather than excusing or condoning the frailties of the beloved.

Why fathers and not mothers? Certainly some women were as important to Manfred's growth as the men in these essays — his mother, wife, and daughters, Meridel LeSueur, Willa Cather, the Aunt Katherine whose life is portrayed in *Eden Prairie* and *Green Earth*. He is an admirer of women, a feminist of his own stamp, proud of the literary achievements of his daughters. It was his father who told him you could only count on two males in a hundred to be good for anything but fattening, but with women it was a surprise if more than two were puny.

Manfred is essentially a whole sexual creature: not a pretentious, swaggering Hemingway; he is a man at peace with his anima rather than threatened by the feminine soul. For prime mothers, read his novels, especially *Green Earth*. These essays are a record of man becoming, and that process may be nurtured by women but it is governed by the male models the boy and youth must face, face down, and break free of. All fathers must lose their sons; Manfred's knew he'd lost his best hired hand to literature before the boy was full grown.

In the most personal of these essays you will find an uneasy balance of truth and love. They will offend some readers, not for their explicitness or their opinions, but with a sudden impact of crudity. That shock should come early, in the sexual banter he reports between himself and Humphrey or the truss comparisons in Muriel Humphrey's living room. If those pass unnoticed, there is the marvelous moment when his father instructs him to reach in and "help the little piglets down the birth canal" and he confesses to us that he found himself "liking what I was doing."

This is Fred Manfred with the hair on, gabby and bold-nosed, telling us things we'd rather not hear, holding back when we'd like to ask questions. What happened, the reader wants to ask, that helped him understand the crazy moment in history when Hugh Glass forgave the two men who left him for dead? He tells us, in "West of the Mississippi," that something happened, but don't pry about the what of it.

Prime Fathers ranges across his nearly fifty years of public life, and yet the eight brief essays lap over one another to laminate and illuminate each other. After you read the personal portrait of Hubert Humphrey dated 1978, you can flip back to the 1943 essay in *The New Republic* where Fred spoke publicly of the friend he admired. The Humphrey essay is classic Manfred, an honest friend's description. Reading it, we see the affection, the private relationship, but the description is whole; without pointing to character flaws, neither does Manfred deny them. The historic Humphrey is here in the friend's eye, filled with glib optimism, sometimes too weak to place intellectual integrity above political loyalty.

Similarly, his two pictures of Sinclair Lewis balance public and personal voice. In an addendum to the essay "Sinclair Lewis: A Portrait," Manfred speaks of the dilemma he faced when asked to give the funeral eulogy for Lewis. The Lewis family wanted the thoughts of another Minnesota writer, some last words in appreciation of a master. But Fred was son, not apprentice. His eulogy says, Fred concluded, what Red Lewis would have wanted — the honest and never simple truth. He speaks of going his own way, bridling strong-headed away from some of Lewis's advice. He calls Lewis a wise father, a man who knew that the young must make their own choices, picking and choosing from what the parent offers. He speaks of his respect and regard for a writer whose gifts were not those Fred Manfred wanted. Nothing in the eulogy suggests the tension that is so obvious in the private portrait, the tension that must have been there from the beginning of their relationship. These essays are about truth, a tough mixture of honest truth and more truth left for the reader to surmise.

The essays mix Manfred's voices effectively, from the chatty, personal Humphrey essay to the elegiac tribute to his father in "Ninety Is Enough," voices of a craftsman attuned to the language of his own Midwest, who captured the staccato energy of Lewis and the native intelligence of turn-of-the-century Iowa farmers who find homilies in pig breeding. It was his father, one of those farmers, who captured the writer's task in a simple observation. Dying in an old folks' home, he lamented that he had no one to talk to, no cronies who wanted to hear a story again "because they saw it too." The storytellers defy time by letting us see it too; they make it first-hand, and each hearing is "again."

There is even a transcript of an extemporaneous speech that captured Manfred's speaking voice, the casual craft of the natural storyteller expanding on his favorite subjects. Anyone who has seen the old Viking holding forth — the gesturing hand, big enough to palm a basketball, curled in what might be lazy repose or the cup that clasps pencil to paper — can hear him in the cadence and humor of that speech and wish for more.

There are scraps here for the Manfred scholar: a biographical hint that illuminates a portion of *King of Spades*; the story of Lewis's escaping spirit in a puff of steam from a funeral urn, which was reworked for the burial of Cain Hammett in *Riders of Judgment*; another reminder that the student of Manfred's style should find out more about Charles Montague Doughty; and three sharp observations that tell us a great deal about Manfred's artistic values. But this is not a scholar's book; it is Manfred's accounting for the man he became, his acknowledgment of the fathers he loved and fought to free himself from, the fathers he complimented by going his own way. And it is a record of an American author whose career has always moved with the force of stone.

Fifteen years ago, Wallace Stegner called Frederick Manfred "an elemental force," and I've heard that phrase behind me whenever I think of the man. But the force is not hurricane or flood. In his own introduction to this book, Manfred talks of making the "ornery cuss" an institution, and his Sinclair Lewis is the quintessential dissenter, noisily acerbic, prickly as pine. The essays themselves celebrate the "aginer," but there is a type stronger and more enduring still, subtler in dissent, and the gaunt old artificer with his young man's juices is its epitome.

Prime Fathers shows us man becoming, the nurturing of a Mark Twain man, upright and unshakeable in his art. Old as oak, grand as ice-scored granite, young as the canyon bed of the Colorado and as deep in his way, old lizard and pure man, not idol, icon or institution but glint-eyed meat and marrow-rich bone, gaunt Moon Dreamer not patriarch, prime father.

— Mick McAllister

*In memory of my
wonderfully independent
grandfather,
Feike Feikes Feikema V*

Wanted:
More Ornery Cusses

What's Happened to the Old-Time Dissenters, Aginers, the Go-It-Aloners?

MODERN LIFE IS HONING EVEN THE ROUGHEST AND TOUGHEST OF US DOWN to nice round, smooth stones. Slowly but surely those interesting little knobs and corners the Good Lord gave us at birth are being ground off.

And now, with the coming of the W-bomb, which can destroy all of us if a single one of us slips, the pressure to conform is really on. We're told in no uncertain terms that we're simply going to have to pack down together, neatly and in rows, or die.

All this is very sad. Because packed, down, we'll die too.

* * *

As an antidote to either extreme, physical death or spiritual death, or both, I have a suggestion to make:

Let's start a cult in which we make heroes out of such ornery cusses as we may still have around — out of our lone wolves, go-it-a-loners, dissenters, hermits, screwballs, aginers. Such a fad, the fad of the ornery cuss or the odd ball, might save us. It is still a truth that the health of a society can be measured by the size and the vigor of its minority group.

In fact, I'd like to recommend that every village and town go out of its way to make sure it still has an ornery cuss in its midst. At least one. And should any village discover it doesn't have an honorable dissenter around, I'd like to suggest that the mayor declare a state of emergency until such a citizen can be found.

1

Because the town atheist, the local aginer, the curmudgeon living on the wrong side of the tracks is exactly the man to keep the town council fairly honest, and the prices in line, and the justice of the peace a justice in fact. Every time I run across a Robert Ingersoll, a Thorstein Veblen, a Eugene Debs, a Harold Ickes, or a Norman Thomas, I say to myself: "Ah, Good! For all its faults, my country is still alive. It will survive. It can still look at both sides of a question."

In my field, writing, I am pleased to note that, despite censorminded busybodies and wolfpack critics and desperate publishers, we still have a few ornery cusses around who refuse to be honed down, who refuse to pack down into piles of indistinguishable stones.

I glory in a solitary William Faulkner who, dedicated and tough, says to himself: "I want it this way or nothing."

I delight in a fierce old Ambrose Bierce who could hate with the best of them in a fine wholesome way. I delight in a Nelson Algren who persists in believing he can find humanity in a sparrow. I glory in the "colossal gall" of a Mark Twain who used the American vernacular in his prose instead of deadcat, conventional English.

I delight in a Sinclair Lewis who could prod a Babbitt into having a private as well as a public conscience. I delight in a fuming Philip Wylie who can throw rocks at Mom; in a corrosive Henry L. Mencken who could call boobs by their right names; in a Fred Babcock who, dedicated to midland culture, can prick the east with its windy claim that it is the true citadel of American culture.

Round rolling stones eventually grind themselves down to fine sand. Who would lose himself in the sands of the sea? Better to have rough corners, and sharp edges, and refuse to budge or roll, and glint in the sun, and even gather gray lichen, and so maybe, with luck, be considered a landmark.

PRIME FATHERS

Hubert Horatio Humphrey
A Memoir

I WAS LIVING IN DINKYTOWN NEAR THE UNIVERSITY OF MINNESOTA in Minneapolis. It was 1938 and I was a reporter for the *Minneapolis Journal*. One evening I walked over to see some friends, Zebe Lumb and Ralph Craft, in a nearby rooming house across the street from Marshall high school. The three of us had the year before roomed together in another house a block further north. I was curious to see how they were getting along. Both were students at the University.

We were talking about the old days back home, Zebe and Ralph about their Webster, South Dakota, and I about Doon, Iowa, when the door opened and a slim dark-haired fellow poked his head in and asked, "You guys busy?" Then he spotted me. "Oh, you have company." The fellow had a high forehead and quick dark blue eyes.

"Come on in, Pinkie," Zebe said. "What the heck, we're just gabbing here. This long-geared gink is an old roomie of ours, Fred Feikema. Fred, this is Hubert Humphrey." With a little laugh, Zebe added, "Pink's from Doland, a suburb of Webster."

"What're you talking about," Hubert laughed back. "Doland isn't even in the same county."

Zebe had a big round red face, full of country apology. "Well, actually, Fred, our Pink now hails from Huron where his father has a drugstore. Doland is where he grew up as a boy."

Ralph was a grave quiet fellow with gray eyes. "For that matter, Zebe, not even Wallace is a suburb."

"What's Wallace?" I asked.

"It's where Hubert was born."

We fell into more easy talk about country towns. It didn't take Hubert long to find out the essentials about me, my home town, where I lived presently, where I worked. I could feel his eyes going over me like an auctioneer's at a farm sale. Within moments the talk got around to the Newspaper Guild, of which I was an active member, and then he knew I was of a liberal cast of mind. That set off a long bull session on politics.

Hubert extolled the virtues of President Franklin Delano Roosevelt and the New Deal. Hubert thought FDR would go down in history as a great man. I said I didn't think so. I'd voted for FDR but wasn't a great admirer of his. I didn't think he was a deep man, certainly not a Washington or a Lincoln. Or for that matter a Woodrow Wilson. "Well," Hubert countered, "there's at least this to be said for FDR — he knew how to get the best brains together and tap them for the good of the country. FDR might not be brainy himself but he knew brains when he saw them."

We four talked until late, until Hubert remembered that he had a wife Muriel who would be wondering where he had been all that time.

After Hubert left, Zebe asked, "What'd you think of him?"

"He sure can talk," I said.

"Yeh, Pinkie always did have a gift of gab." It was obvious that Zebe admired Hubert very much.

Ralph smiled quietly to himself, head held to one side a little. "Yes, Pinkie gets a little high-flown once in a while. But he knows what he's talking about. Terribly bright man."

Hubert intrigued me, and shortly after I'd met him I made it a point to go visit him. From Zebe and Ralph I learned Hubert was working his way through the University as a pharmacist at the Brown Drug across the campus on Washington Avenue. I'd go in and buy a malted milk and then sit joshing with him for a while. He had a curious way of doing two things at the same time, a quick eye out for a customer that might drop by at the same time that he kept up a running argument with me. Sometimes I was taken aback by the way he could be overly polite with a customer one moment and then the next moment argue intensely with me. As a boy from the country I'd always looked askance at store clerks with asslicking manners.

Besides fretting over what the New Deal was doing to our economy, both of us were also quite worried about what Hitler was doing to Germany and to the balance of power in Europe. We spoke gloomily of the possibility of another World War. In any case, no matter how vigorously we might argue with each other, our discussions always ended with a warm handshake and a warm smile, and with the promise that we'd soon see each other to continue the gabfests.

In 1939, Hubert went down to Baton Rouge to get his masters degree in political science at Louisiana State University, and I didn't get to see him again for four years. During that interval, I lost my job at the *Journal.* Later on, due to lack of regular meals, and exposure to two families with miliary tuberculosis, I broke down with tuberculosis, recuperated in the Glen Lake Sanatorium for two years, lived in a rest home for several months, and finally took a job with *Modern Medicine* as an abstractor for some six months.

Then in April of 1943, the phone rang in our home around nine o'clock. I was already in bed with my wife Maryanna. Both of us had made it a point to go to bed early to make sure we stayed healthy, since she too had spent two years in the Glen Lake Sanatorium. The phone rang and rang, and finally I got up and answered it. Arthur Naftalin was on the phone and wanted to know if I could drop over to a friend's house for a bull session. Art and I had been friends on the campus of the University of Minnesota before I'd become ill. I'd been a reporter and he'd taken journalism, and we'd often bumped into each other at parties.

"Who's the friend?" I asked.

"Hubert Humphrey."

"Hey, I know him."

"Sure, and he says he knows you. Could you come over? It's kind of important."

"I'll see what my wife says."

My wife grumbled a little, but she really was too sleepy to protest much. I wondered a little what her real thoughts about me were as I left to visit with "some of the boys." It would be my first time out alone since we'd been married.

I drove over to Hubert's house in southeast Minneapolis, not too far from Dinkytown. It was a modest two-story house, with a neat yard, and when I entered I found the living room equally neat. The two children were already in bed. An old-fashioned stand-up dark mahogany radio stood in one corner, with a toy dog and cat on it. The furniture was of the dark brown plush type, big chair and davenport, all neatly arranged, with a dark rug underfoot.

Art greeted me in his usual chary manner. For a young man he'd always had an old wise smile. "You know Hubert, of course."

Hubert and I shook hands warmly, exclaiming how good it was to see each other again.

Art said, "And this is Evron Kirkpatrick, of the Political Science Department at the U." Art added that he too was now in political science.

I shook hands with a man who had light blond hair, a square face, and penetrating light-blue eyes. I realized right away that Evron was a man who on the outside might appear to be a quiet modest fellow but who on the inside had a racing-swift shrewd mind. Evron was not one to wear his emotions on his sleeve.

Hubert broke in at this point. "And this is my wife Muriel, Fred."

Muriel had a soft South Dakota smile, brown hair parted in the middle, done up in waves. One could see that she used curlers.

"Well," Hubert said, "have a chair, Freddie. Take a load off your feet."

We talked at random for a while. There was some catching up to do. Muriel went to get some coffee and doughnuts. Presently Muriel retired.

I picked up a second doughnut and turned to Art. "Well, what was so important that you had to rouse me out of a warm bed and have me leave behind a sweet wife?"

"Hubert is thinking of running for mayor," Art said. "Some labor leaders want him to run. Do you think he can make it?"

"Which labor people?"

"AF of L."

"That won't be enough."

"That's what we think. And that's why we asked you over. You were once a member of the Newspaper Guild, weren't you, and through them got to know some of the CIO people?" Art had often talked to me about politics and labor relations. "Do you think Hubert can win them over?"

I had heard how Hubert, as director of the Workers' Education Program, had fired some teachers who weren't pulling their weight. Some of them had been leftwingers who'd spent much of their work time organizing protest meetings instead of teaching. The left-wingers had been enraged. Many of them were friends of the CIO labor leaders. I said, "Art, it's going to be tough titty."

"That's where we thought you'd come in. You know them from the old days when you were a reporter and maybe they'd listen to you."

"I can try. But I'll tell you something. Winning the CIO over isn't going to be enough either."

We talked until early in the morning, going over all the problems. Finally I told Art that I thought Hubert could win. I hadn't yet heard him give a speech, but friends had told me that he was a first-rate spellbinder. Besides, I loved to take chances, big ones. Also several times in the past, both before and after Governor Floyd B. Olson died, I myself had been approached to run for a political office. Roman Becker, an editor for the old Farmer-Labor paper *The Leader*, had wanted me to run for state legislature, first as a representative, then as a senator, and slowly build up a reputation until I'd be ripe to run for governor. Becker had heard me one night arguing eloquently with some professors.

A day or so later, Hubert took the plunge. He filed for office of mayor of the city of Minneapolis.

We had a hectic time. It was assumed that Mayor Marvin Kline would easily win first spot in the primaries. For second place, Hubert had to beat out eight other candidates, among them, T. A. Eide, perennial labor candidate, and Luke Rader, a rabble-rousing evangelist who'd decided to run and clean up the city. Eide was a prominent leader in the cooperative movement and Rader had his own radio show.

Hubert was like a whirlwind. He was everywhere at once it seemed. And he beat out both Eide and Rader, coming in 13,477 votes behind Kline.

Hubert set up campaign headquarters on Hennepin and Ninth. Two women from labor leader Harold Seavey's office manned the telephone and the reception desk. The rest of us, Art, Evron, Hubert, and myself, scurried all over town with our leaflets. Sometimes when Hubert couldn't quite make a speaking engagement, we'd fill in. Art and Evron were good at it. I wasn't.

Hubert soon learned that I knew the city quite well. As a one-time reporter for the *Journal* I'd made it a point to know where every street was. Art and Evron had their duties on the campus and couldn't always be around. So gradually I was the one who rode with Hubert everywhere in his car. I was supposed to be his driver but he was too impatient to let me drive and I wound up sitting in front with him, listening to him expound on one thing or another.

Still Hubert could be a good listener. I researched for meetings he was scheduled to address. For the Townsend Club, for example, I dug up material on the founder, Francis W. Townsend, who believed in giving pensions to old people for them to spend within a month to speed up the use of money. Filled in, Hubert would take the few facts I gave him and make a dramatic flourishing talk.

On another occasion I took him to a practice session of the Minneapolis Symphony Orchestra in Northrup auditorium. I boned up on what the orchestra would be playing at its next concert, and provided Hubert with some background on both the musical selections and the composers. Hubert walked in and instantly noticed they weren't too excited about seeing him. Dmitri Mitropoulos, the conductor, barely had time for him. But Hubert took the background material I'd given him and gave one of the best ten-minute impromptu talks on music I ever heard. When he finished, the musicians gave him the ultimate in ovations by lightly tapping their bows on the strings of their instruments; and Dmitri went over to Hubert, threw his arms around him, and gave him a Grecian kiss.

My wife Maryanna, meanwhile, had been taking a pretty dim view of my sudden interest in politics. As she often said, politics was about the last thing she'd ever been interested in. And she was amazed that I, a man who wanted to be a writer, a man who loved solitude, had suddenly become so active in public affairs and traveled around with "a would-be politician."

Then one evening Maryanna met him. We had been invited to a small supper party at which Hubert was to speak. Frederick Kottke and William Kubicek were hosts. Everybody but Hubert was there on time. This caused quite a laugh. Hubert's reputation for always being a little late was growing rapidly. He just couldn't resist adding a second conclusion and a third conclusion to any speech he gave. Also, he loved people and couldn't tear himself away when someone wanted to tell him the sorry tale of their lives or give him some sage advice on how to handle the worthy opponent.

Finally he arrived with Muriel, he chipper and quick-moving and greeting everybody at once, Muriel demure and apologetic. The room was instantly galvanized by his presence. It was like magic to see what had been somewhat desultory talk suddenly become excited talk. When he looked at you he looked at you directly, piercingly, with those dark blue eyes, to your core, and it always made you jump, made you want to do something, promise something, get something done. And before an evening was over he usually got in that look at every one. Dialogue quickened; laughter deepened; wit flashed. Soon the talk turned political and then Vesuvius took over.

On the way home that night my wife said, her face alive and her eyes sparkling from the lively evening, "Well, I've just met a man who's going to be the president of our country some day. You were right. He is an exceptional man."

As assistant campaign manager I was called on to do some

strange things. We had some difficulty, for example, in reaching Bill Mauseth, CIO leader in Minneapolis. He was known as the king of the leftwingers (an odd title for a revolutionary) who pretty well dictated the politics of his union. When I called him on the telephone, he was always out, not available. Finally I suggested to Hubert that he just go barge into the CIO headquarters and keep asking for Mauseth until he got hold of him. Hubert was game and we drove over. But when we got there it was as though they'd had advance notice we were coming, as though they had a spy in our midst. The offices were empty except for a couple of girl clerks. Well, for Hubert two people was a crowd, and he proceeded to lecture them on the issues of the mayoralty campaign. The girls tried to voice their objections to what he was saying but he overwhelmed them with his rhetoric and his pointing finger. For myself I thought he was overdoing it a bit. It was as if Hubert felt that if he could properly indoctrinate the two girl clerks they in turn could influence others in the CIO ranks. He had to get that CIO vote.

This went on for about five minutes — when abruptly a little sliding pass-through door in a wall opened and through it popped Bill Mauseth's head. Mauseth's face was all worked up. He had been listening on the other side of the wall. "That's all very well, Hubert," he rasped, "but what about the international situation, ha?" Mauseth meant, of course, what was Hubert's attitude toward the USSR.

Hubert, astonished to see Mauseth's face in the pass-through opening, reared back a step, flashed a look at me as if to say, "My God, Freddie, what kind of place have you brought me to?" . . . then, recovering, and re-presenting his pointing finger, shot back, "Mr. Mauseth, I doubt that as mayor of Minneapolis I'll be very much concerned with any international dealings with Russia. The really important issue is this: do you want a good mayor in the office here who'll clean up the city, get rid of gambling, prostitution, and all underworld connections? Or do you want to continue with Marvin Kline as your mayor and have a wide open town? And furthermore, don't you want a mayor in office who for once will give a fair shake to the labor movement?"

The two of them went at it a good quarter of an hour, with Mauseth trying to swing the argument around to how Hubert felt about the Communists, and with Hubert continually emphasizing the need for clean government.

Mauseth finally gave up. Actually. He slowly pulled back his head and closed the little sliding pass-through door. And again, after a moment, somewhat reluctantly, he came around by the regular door and shook hands with Hubert. It was my turn to be astounded. I'd heard that Mauseth wasn't much for shaking hands, unless it was with a very good comrade.

The campaign committee was broke all the time. We were always short of money: for postage, for posters, for campaign literature. Hubert was such an unknown that it was hard to get backing. Also, Hubert was picky about where the money came from.

I remember one mysterious call I took at the headquarters. The man on the other end of the phone, who at first wouldn't give his name, suggested that he could get a $10,000 campaign contribution for Hubert, but he wanted a certain understanding with Hubert first. I finally got the man's name and his telephone number. I reported it to Hubert. Hubert was instantly on the alert and told me to investigate it further.

The fellow lived near the corner of 18th Street and Third Avenue South in a sleazy apartment with smelly overstuffed furniture. He'd told me to come over late in the evening but I decided to pop in on him in the morning. I'd gathered that he was a night owl and I figured his thinking would be slower in the morning than in the evening. While I myself was best in the morning. I rapped on his door around nine A.M. He didn't want to answer the door at first and was irritated as hell when he discovered who it was. He had the sniffing manners of a wary old corncrib rat. He shuffled into his clothes and poured himself some cold black coffee, desperately trying to wake up.

It took him a while to get to the point. But at last, coughing, working hard to clear his head, he finally told me that he and his bunch wanted to have the right to name the chief of police for that $10,000 contribution. Hubert could run the city any way he wanted to except for that. The chief of police had to be their man. I kept a good poker face, but inside kept wondering who this fellow's "bunch" might be. And at last my stratagem of rousing him out of bed when he was at his sleepiest paid off. He let slip "they" were out of Chicago.

I thanked him, said I'd let him know, and left. I went back to the campaign headquarters and reported to Hubert.

Hubert was outraged. "We won't even bother to get back to them. You hear?"

On another occasion Gideon Seymour, executive editor of the *Minneapolis Star*, called me. I'd been in to see him several times about a job, and had met him at parties around town. He was a portly man with a heavy flushed face. After some hemming and hawing, and making sure that I wouldn't go tattling around town, he finally told me what he had in mind. "I think I can raise $500 for Hubert. From the Dayton boys and some other fat cat friends at the Athletic Club. They are willing to take up a collection."

"A whole five hundred?" I managed not to let sarcasm creep into my voice.

"Yes. Hubert can use it, can't he? We hear he is hard up for funds."

I almost laughed outloud. It meant the fat cats were beginning to worry Hubert might win and they wanted to make a side bet to get in on the game. I told Gideon I'd talk it over with Hubert. "Hubert is mighty careful about where he gets his money."

"I know he is and that's why we like him."

It made me wonder a little if Gideon knew about the rejected $10,000 offer.

About that same time, a man who identified himself as Kelly called me one evening. After some throat clearing, he indicated he and his friends wanted to help Hubert win too. Would Hubert be interested? I'd just had a nap and still wasn't altogether clear-headed. But as we talked it hit me that I'd met the man at the same party where I'd met Bill Mauseth and other leftwingers, along with some artists and writers. Kelly was a Communist. He ended by saying, "We think Hubert has a good chance to win. And we want to help put him over. Also, we think we can help his thinking on certain social-oriented matters."

I reported that call to Hubert too. He almost snorted. "That would be the kiss of death. Stay away from them."

Gene Williams, one of the leaders in the Teamsters Union, liked Hubert and wanted to help him. Williams suggested that if Hubert could print up some postcards with a pointed message the postcards could be run through the Teamsters' addressing machine. There were some two thousand members. Hubert thought that a great idea. It was bound to pick up a few extra votes. He'd been hearing around town that, while the AF of L was completely behind his campaign, the Teamsters were dragging their feet. Hubert assigned the job of running those postcards through the addressing machine to me. Evron helped me carry the cards over from our headquarters on Hennepin to the Teamsters headquarters on First Avenue North across the street from the Greyhound bus depot. The two girls from our office came along to help run the machine.

We were about finished addressing the cards, when the door burst open and in tromped Fritz Snyder and several other Teamster goons. Fritz was known as a brawler of nightspots. I'd met Fritz once before. As a member of the Newspaper Guild I'd helped on the picket line when the WTCN radio news staff went on strike. The Local 544 goon squad wanted to run the engineers, who were AF of L, through our CIO Newspaper Guild picket line at the WTCN transmitter. Our Guild members were augmented by the CIO meatpackers of South St. Paul, a notoriously tough bunch, and it looked like there was going to be a real showdown. Rather than have general bloodshed, I suggested that a champion be selected from each side and have them fight it out. Fritz was chosen for the 544 side and I was chosen for the Guild side. (I was a sports reporter at the time and it was known I'd also done some boxing.) Luckily, just as we were taking off our jackets and shirts and were bare down to the belt, a man came running from the WTCN transmitter to tell us the strike was settled.

Fritz was a huge man, well over six feet and built like a super wedge. I was taller but he was heavier. He and his couple of boys bore down on us where we were running the addressing machine. He ordered us to stop the machine and told his boys to grab the postcards already addressed.

"What's the trouble?" I exclaimed. "Williams told us we could use this machine."

"He don't know from nothin'," Fritz said. "Besides, he ain't the real boss. Shut off that machine!"

The rumor that the Teamsters were dragging their feet proved to be right.

I'd always regretted that I hadn't had that tangle with Fritz, just to show him that brawlers can't always have their way. I decided to front up to him, and with a little Siouxland smile to disarm him I stepped up to him. I could see that he was wearing a gun, as were his buddies. I said, "Look, Fritz, I'm not packing a gun. See?" With both hands I opened wide my suit jacket. "So I'm no match for you." I reached forward and patted his chest, and then, easy does it, flipped back the left side of his jacket to reveal a shoulder holster and gun. "Now, you don't really want to scare my girls with that thing, do you?" I turned to look for Evron to include him in the dialogue, only to discover he'd disappeared. When I glanced back at the girls, I could see that, if they already didn't have wet panties, they sure as heck were going to have them soon. I gestured behind my back for the girls to keep running those cards through the addressing machine.

Fritz was taken off guard. He blinked and stood hesitating.

"Fritz, remember that time on the picket line? When we almost went for each other?"

Fritz nodded. Out of the corner of his eye he watched the addressing machine pump out more cards. "Yeh, but . . . . Look, we had orders to grab them postcards of yours."

"Maybe we should have that go-round after all. Of course, I'm going to have to ask you to strip down to your waist, like that other time. And I'll do the same." I began to take off my jacket. I knew that in any case a jacket was a bad thing to be wearing in a fight. All the other fellow has to do is jerk your jacket back by the collar and he has your arms pinned.

"Naw," Fritz said, "I don't wanna fight you. We just want them cards, is all. We had orders."

I kept putting him off with more palaver and he kept hesitating.

Finally, I heard the last postcard drop out of the addressing machine. I shut off the machine and picked up the big box in which all the cards lay neatly stacked. With a nod at the girls I indicated they could go. They grabbed their purses and skedaddled. I was left alone with Fritz and his two boys. With the box under one arm, and gesturing amicably, I started for the door in as casual a manner as I could muster. Fritz and his buddies followed me, Fritz arguing all the while that he had had orders and it would be his neck if those postcards got mailed.

I kept joshing them as we went down the stairs, and then outdoors onto the sidewalk. I remembered that there was a big mailbox on the corner across from the entrance to the bus depot. I made it a point not to look at the mailbox at the same time that I gradually eased over to the side of the walk where it stood. Then, before they knew what was happening, I opened the big mouth of the mailbox and dumped the whole load of postcards in it.

"There, boys, if you want those postcards back, go after them. But remember, if you dig them out of that mailbox, it'll be a federal offense."

Fritz stomped and cursed and threatened the air, but he didn't quite dare to pull his gun.

I stepped across the street and headed for the Humphrey headquarters. Once out of sight of Fritz and his buddy goons, I broke out in a cold sweat. And wondered where in God's name I'd got the guts to do what I'd just done.

When I showed up at the headquarters, Hubert heaved a huge sigh of relief. Evron had filled him in about what had happened. Evron was white, and angry. The two girls, I learned, had on arrival headed straight for the ladies' room and were still in there. Hubert commended me but he said he wasn't sure we needed all that bravery.

Most times Evron and Art and I got along well. Evron and Art, as University of Minnesota political scientists, were a little heavy on the strategy side and not very heavy on the actual work side. Evron and Art felt they were too valuable as thinkers to be distributing leaflets door to door, which I did, when I wasn't driving Hubert around.

But we clashed one day when it turned out that Art had scheduled a luncheon meeting with some businessmen for Hubert, cancelling out a meeting that I'd set up with the difficult CIO. I still wasn't sure about CIO support but I felt a few more visits with the leaders would help. I got up from my chair. "Hubert, the heck with the businessmen. Besides, I promised the CIO boys you'd come and you better be there." I spoke with some force. Torn between an old loyalty to Art and Evron, and my show of some anger, Hubert didn't know what to do. But finally he sailed out the door with Art, and he did it with a look over his shoulder as if he were afraid of me. His leaving so sheepishly really did make me feel disgusted. I had been drawn into the whole thing in the first place to help him get CIO support.

I didn't remain angry very long. Like Hubert, I never could stay angry. Besides, he was such a lovable fellow, with his endless cheer, his indomitable force, his witty greetings, his endless concern for the welfare of his workers.

Herbert McCloskey, also from the Department of Political Science at the University of Minnesota, sometimes helped out. He wrote some of Hubert's radio speeches. McCloskey and I often argued about these scripts. McCloskey always approached his subject matter as if everything he wrote had to be on a par with Plato's *Republic*. His writing wound up, of course, being very heavy, loaded with polysyllabics. Two minutes into the speech and there'd be nobody listening. I tried to jazz up the language a little, after McCloskey got through with his draft, but that made McCloskey angry. So I finally told Hubert to quit reading the McCloskey scripts, and to speak extemporaneously. Hubert was ten times better talking off the cuff than anything either McCloskey or I wrote for him. Twice I threw McCloskey's drafts away, after jotting down the gist of them, and told Hubert to take it from there. Hubert was impressive when he talked extemporaneously. Curiously enough, Hubert, otherwise too long-winded, always managed to confine his remarks to the time slot allotted him.

With two weeks to go, Mayor Kline began to worry that Hubert was gaining on him. Kline, on the advice of his secretary Frank Mayer, decided to hit out at Hubert. In one of his campaign speeches he called Hubert a political upstart who made promises he could never deliver on. He claimed Hubert was guilty of making misstatements if not telling lies. Kline's remarks made the front page of the *Star* and the *Tribune*.

Art and Evron were dumbfounded. And Hubert was angry. They debated what to do about it. Hubert had to strike back somehow.

I said, "Hubert, I know what I'd do if I was running."

"What's that, Freddie?"

"He's calling you a liar, isn't he?"

"Well, yes, I guess he is."

"I'd never let anybody call me a liar, political campaign or not. Not even President Roosevelt."

"You mean, you'd go see him personally?"

"You bet I'd go see him personally. I'd barge right into Mayor Kline's office, mad as a hornet, and challenge him to prove his allegations."

"Gee, I don't know . . . ."

"Hubert, if you'll go over there, right now, I'll see to it that some reporters and photographers will be on hand to witness it all. That'll really make the front pages."

Art and Evron weren't sure either that my idea was such a good one. Because of that Fritz Snyder episode of mine, they were already a little wary about some of my suggestions.

"Hubert," I said, "until now the newspapers haven't given you much space. They've assumed all along that Kline will win easily, that you really aren't newsworthy. Well, you beard that fellow in his own den, the mayor's office, and point your finger at him, and hit him with a blunt face-to-face challenge, you'll get coverage like you've never had before."

Hubert gave it some more thought; finally said, "All right, Freddie, you call up your newspaper friends and Art you come along with me."

Hubert did get attention. Front page. Kline, totally startled, was almost speechless. The only trouble was, after the confrontation, some reporter suggested that the two shake hands. Well, you know Hubert. He never could carry a legitimate grudge longer than a minute or so. Hubert shook hands with Kline. The handshake was photographed and it defused the point of his dramatic visit. But it made news.

Every now and then Hubert would come flying into the office of a morning, take a good look around, and then shake his head over all the clutter underfoot, the kind of clutter all campaign headquarters collect: torn posters, old newspapers, folders, leaflets, cards. He'd grab a broom and sweep up the place. He had a curious way of skipping about as he worked. Soon everybody caught the spirit and helped clean up. "You see, my friends," he'd say, "that's the way I want people to see me. That I like to clean things up. Just like I intend to clean up the city of Minneapolis."

Several times while visiting his home, I saw Hubert glance around at his living room and decide there was too much clutter about there too. He wouldn't complain to Muriel, but instead would go to the broom closet, and actually, with company present, neat up the joint. Muriel always smiled quietly to herself as she watched him bustle about, and went on doing whatever it was she was busy with, washing dishes, changing diapers.

He was the same way with his clothes. He was always dressed neat, dapper. His tie was always in place. He was always cleanly shaven. And his haircuts had to be just right. He was a man who as a boy had been trained to meet the public with his best foot forward.

When anybody showed up at the campaign headquarters, Hubert would invariably be the first to greet the stranger. Hubert was not one to sit in the back office, inaccessible to the public, thinking deep thoughts about the issues, but was always out front. He had the typical shopkeeper's philosophy — serve the customer immediately. For myself I wasn't always sure I wanted to meet every Tom, Dick, and Harry that dropped in. I wasn't a natural glad-hander. When I asked Hubert where he got that trait, he had a ready answer: "Working for my father in his drugstore. When you have a shop, you better be prepared to give the customer service. Right now. And do it with a smile."

Later on this work ethic served Hubert well. He became known for the promptness with which he answered his mail, both as mayor of Minneapolis and as United States senator. Even conservative farmers had to admit, grudgingly, that they got quicker service from Hubert's office than they did from their own Republican senator.

One weekend shortly before the general election Hubert announced that he and his friend Orville Freeman were going out on the town for the evening to have some fun, just the two of them. I showed surprise, thinking he'd be glad he could at last stay home one night with wife and children. Hubert caught my look. "Well, Freddie, my dad taught me a number of things, and one of them was to make the women in the house understand we men weren't always slaveys. Dad said that every now and then we men have got to break free of the women, wives, mothers, sisters, daughters, and have a night out with the boys." There was a hint in the way Hubert said it that should the boys decide to see other women, well, that too according to Hubert's father was a man's privilege. I was very much in love with my wife at the time and had trouble understanding that philosophy. Furthermore, I'd always been somewhat of a feminist, believing that what was fair for the men should also be fair for the women.

A few days before the election, Hubert's brother Ralph and his wife drove up for what was to be a victory celebration. Ralph was helping his father run the Humphrey Drugstore in Huron. Ralph was a bluff man, full of wisecracks, with a quiet, almost hard, eye for the passing show. He liked to goad Hubert and the two of them were constantly challenging each other.

One evening the subject came up as to why Hubert wasn't in the armed forces, helping his country fight the Germans and the Japanese. The question of Hubert being a draft dodger had been raised several times by the Kline camp. Ralph in turn taunted Hubert with it. Hubert said he'd tried several times to enlist but neither the army nor navy would take him. He had a bad hernia.

"Oh, hell, Pink," Ralph said, "your hernia ain't all that bad. While me now, man, I've really got one. In fact, my hernia is so bad it looks like I've got an extra appendage there."

"G'wan, Ralph," Hubert said. "When it comes right down to it, mine's the worst. I've got a double hernia. Two of 'em."

At this point both wives, sitting in Hubert's living room listening to the combative talk, woke up. Such kind of talk was going a little too far, they said, especially with company present. I was the company.

But Ralph was not to be outdone. "I'll show you," he said. He promptly unbuckled his belt and lowered his trousers and his shorts to reveal he was wearing a truss, and that the truss was holding back a considerable protuberance.

With a laugh Hubert followed suit. He slipped down his suspenders and lowered his trousers and shorts to reveal a truss. His was a double truss. I hadn't known he wore such a device. So that accounted for his odd skipping walk. He worked his legs directly off his hip joints. Because of the truss he couldn't let his whole body flow into his walk.

The two men standing there with shorts and trousers lowered to almost half-mast was a sight to behold. There was a lot of laughter.

Muriel decided things had gone far enough. "All right, you two, if you must show off your torsos, into the bathroom with you. Shame on you."

Hubert almost won election. He lost only because of his honesty. One of his last talks was before the Bartenders Union. He gave his usual rousing speech. At the end he asked for questions from the audience. One question proved to be his undoing. Someone asked him, "Is it true, Mr. Humphrey, that if you get elected, you're going to close down the town?"

Hubert shot back, "Yessir, tight as a drum. I'm sick of hearing that Minneapolis is a two-time town — in the day a sleepy conservative financial center, at night a wide open town for gambling, prostitution, and liquor."

Nothing more was said at the meeting. But afterwards, from then until the election, every bartender in town made it a point to tell his customers that if they voted for Hubert they wouldn't be able to have a beer on their way home from work or an occasional night out on the town with the boys.

Hubert lost by just 5,725.

Sometime during the summer of 1943, after Hubert got a job teaching at Macalester College, he dropped by my house for a visit. I was living at 1814 4th Street, S. E., at the time. We sat in my study in the back of the house, first floor. I'd gone back to my writing. The walls of my den were lined with books and I'd built myself both a slanting writing desk and a typing stand and was raring to go.

We reviewed the campaign and had some good laughs together about it.

Finally Hubert got around to why he'd come to see me. "Freddie, right now, so long as I work for Macalester, I'm not supposed to be politicking. The fact is, though, politics is my life, and I'm going to run for mayor again in two years. But the next time around it's going to be different. I want you to be my right hand man. Art and Evron are okay, you know, great friends of mine. But they really are a little too academic. Labor leaders don't like that university crowd and I need the support of labor to win. Besides, I noticed in the last campaign that you were willing to get out and pound the streets and ring doorbells and peddle leaflets. You were willing to go see Mauseth with me. You went into that Teamsters den that time. A real precinct worker. You not only know how to read many different kinds of people, you also get along with them. You know the man in the street, and I'm sure you know the man in the country, coming as you do from the country. You have a down to earth way with people. So look, Freddie, you work with me and we'll someday go to Washington, D. C. together."

I was glad my wife wasn't listening. She already had a premonition of the kind of hard life I was going to have as a writer. She would have urged me to go with Hubert, and if I still wanted to write, do it in my spare time.

Hubert went on. "And the best thing is, Freddie, you and I get along. We understand each other instantly. Maybe it's because we both come from the sticks. You were raised around Doon, Iowa, and I was raised in Doland, South Dakota. Let's work together. What do you say?"

I am easily moved. Too often I've let people persuade me to get into things I afterwards regret. And Hubert with his very persuasive personality, his winning infectious manner, was hard to resist. Somehow, though, I for once stubborned up inside. I knew one thing absolutely for sure — I'd never be happy in politics, or for that matter in any kind of public life. I'd had a taste of it with him in the election just past, and I hadn't liked it at all. I was a private man. I liked my privacy. I liked working at my desk of judgment.

"What do you say, Freddie?"

"Hubert, I'm sorry, but really, I'm not all that hot about politics. I'm not good with crowds. I don't like crowds. I love sitting alone here working at my novels. I've already got three written, you know, various drafts of them, and my head is full of other ideas for books. If I don't get them all down, and published, I'd feel terrible later on in life. Like I'd betrayed some kind of holy trust given me. So I've got to do them. I'll go crazy if I don't."

Hubert looked at me surprised.

"And anyway, Hubert, for your sake, you and I really shouldn't be seen together as a team. I'm a good six foot nine and you're about six feet. Every time we stepped down out of a train together, or off an airplane, they'd first look at me, and then at you. When you should be the first and only main attraction. Furthermore, seeing my huge bulk, people would begin to think you'd hired yourself a big goon for a bodyguard. No, Hubert, it won't work."

Hubert argued for a while, trying to make me change my mind. But I wouldn't do it.

Very reluctantly, a little sadly, Hubert finally got up to go. It was almost one o'clock. We shook hands, warmly, regretfully, and agreed to keep in touch.

That fall I wrote an article about Minnesota politics. It was accepted by *The New Republic* and was published under the title of "Report From Minnesota," * October 11, 1943. We had a party at our house on Fourth Street the day it arrived in the mail. The Naftalins, Kubiceks, Kottkes, and others from old campaign days were all there. It was to be one of those parties where Hubert would meet privately with his political friends to help keep the Humphrey dream alive. Hubert and Muriel, as usual, were a little late. I saw them coming up the walk, so I went to the door to greet them, and then in the hallway I showed them the article in *The New Republic*. I was quite proud of it. It was my first published piece in a national magazine. It was also the first mention of Hubert in a national magazine. In it I suggested that Humphrey would probably move up the political ladder, while Harold Stassen would go down. Hubert had antennas out for people; Harold did not.

Hubert was delighted to see it, and with his quick eyes glanced through it. Then he handed it to Muriel. Muriel also glanced at it. She wanted to know if any of the company had seen it. I said they hadn't; I'd been saving it for Hubert and Muriel to see first.

We entered the room where the others had been waiting.

Muriel with her quiet smile held up the magazine. "It's in there all right, just as Freddie promised it would be."

There were pleased smiles all around.

(That same article caught the eye of Robert Penn Warren, poet and novelist. Warren called me one afternoon to ask if he couldn't talk to me about it. We agreed first to take a walk and then go to his house on Logan Avenue in Minneapolis and talk. Sitting in his den with a hot buttered rum in hand, Warren explained he was

* See page 117 below.

working on a novel on southern politics. He said he was curious to know what northern politics might be like, on the inside. Of course, Red said, if you're going to use the material yourself, then you shouldn't help me. I told Warren it'd be years before I got around to using what I knew about Hubert, or for that matter about Stassen and the former governor Elmer Benson. By that time, I said, I'd probably have a different slant on what I'd be telling him.)

The next summer I had lunch with Hubert and Art. During the course of some lively male talk, Hubert leaned over to Art, and said with a smile at me, "By the way, Art, Freddie's got one in the oven."

I blushed. It was true that my wife and I were expecting.

A few months later when our first child, Freya, was born, Muriel brought over a supply of used diapers and a bassinet. The Humphreys were in between babies, she said, and didn't need the diapers just then. Hubert and Muriel knew we were hard up. My first novel, *The Golden Bowl*, had gotten fine reviews, but no great sales, and I was struggling to complete my second book, *Boy Almighty*.

When their next child was born, I returned the diapers and the bassinet. I remarked to Muriel that the diapers had by that time become pretty threadbare. They were hardly much better than cheesecloth. But here they were anyway. "Thanks for all your help."

Muriel laughed. "I'll just have to put on two at a time then."

By the time Hubert ran for mayor again, my wife and I had moved out into what was at that time open country in Bloomington, on the bluffs overlooking the Minnesota River, and I couldn't be of much help to him. The next time around Hubert swamped Mayor Marvin Kline.

I visited Hubert in the mayor's office many times. He'd left word with the office help that any time I showed up he was to be told. I was often ushered into his office. Sometimes I sat in on conferences, and after the visitors had left, he'd ask me for my opinion on what I'd seen and heard. I had one piece of advice for him that he never followed. I told him, "Hubert, you read other people's minds so fast you never give them a chance to finish what they've come to say. You take the words right out of their mouth. Hubert, nobody really likes that. Why don't you bite on your tongue and let them finish? Let them think they've told you something important."

Once while in his office talking, the phone rang. It was Muriel. Hubert leaned back in his armchair and listened. He sat silently listening for what seemed at least five minutes. There was a patient indulgent smile on his lips. I gathered it wasn't so much that she was whining or complaining as that she was voicing her wifely concerns about various family matters.

Finally he leaned forward in his chair and brought it all to an end by saying, "Muriel, you know that I'll do what is right, and you know also what that is," and hung up, shaking his head.

For once he had sat back and listened. I sat there wishing he'd do the same thing with labor leaders and other people who came to his office. But a wife has more rights. Also, she'd probably earlier let him know she didn't like for him to take the words right out of her mouth.

On another occasion we got around to talking about our ambitions. He never failed to tell me that someday he was going to go to Washington, D. C., as either a representative or a senator, possibly even as president.

Then, apropos really of nothing we'd talked about, he said, "But you know what's more wonderful than being president?"

"What?"

"To have that thing stand out there stiff and hard and bobbing back and forth. Sex is one of the great immediate joys of life."

I couldn't have agreed more. I was perfectly willing to trade the presidency, which I didn't want in the first place, for a good lively sex life.

When Hubert ran for the United States Senate in 1948 against incumbent Joseph Ball, I campaigned for Hubert as much as I could out on the bluff. I wasn't always well and had to husband my strength for the writing of novels. But I wrote a letter for him to the *Minneapolis Star* that was printed in full. I drew a series of comparisons between Humphrey and Ball and what they stood for. The letter got a lot of attention. Virginia Stafford, for one, then a columnist for the *Star*, called me to say that because of the letter she was going to switch her vote to Hubert. She said many of her friends were going to do the same. Hubert also called me up to thank me. At the end of the conversation he said, "Freddie, that was a wonderful letter, and I still say that if you'd have gone with me, we'd really have climbed the heights together."

A year after he was elected to the U. S. Senate, I was appointed writer in residence at Macalester College. I hadn't been on the job a week when I got a letter of congratulations from Hubert. As a former professor at Macalester he welcomed me to the Macalester ranks.

With him living in Washington, D. C., our lives drifted apart. We kept in touch by writing occasional letters. When the Viet Nam War came along I wrote him to protest the bombing of Hue. The destruction of one of the most beautiful cities in the world, I said, with some of the world's great art in it, was not worth the few North Vietnamese hidden in it. It would have been better to starve them out of it rather than blast them out of it. Except possibly for the work of William Faulkner, we had nothing in the way of an art in our country to match Hue — and that included the Johnson Administration, of which Hubert was a part as vice president.

Hubert wrote right back. "Thanks for the brickbats," he said, and then went on to defend the action in a two-page letter. From the tone of the letter I detected that what he said was not necessarily his own personal point of view.

I wrote him again and suggested he resign as vice president. I told him the young would love him for it, and if he finally wanted a chance at the presidency that was the route to take. He wrote back to say that he'd given it serious thought but felt that there was much to be said for party loyalty.

The last time I saw him in person was at Sauk Centre. Humphrey was the main speaker at the dedication of the Sinclair Lewis Interpretative Center. As an old friend of Red Lewis I had been invited to sit on the speaker's platform. When Hubert arrived he spotted me sitting alone on a corner of the platform waiting for things to begin. He immediately strode over and shook hands.

"What are you doing here?" he asked.

"Paying my respects to an old friend. Russell Fridley, head of the Historical Society, invited me up. And then I wanted to see you again."

He was all smiles and we embraced warmly.

A little later, while the master of ceremonies was introducing the various dignitaries, Hubert got out a sheaf of papers on which he'd earlier scribbled some notes and wrote something in the margin. I found out what that was a few minutes later.

Hubert was well into his speech, lauding Lewis' contribution to Minnesota as a literary giant, when he turned and pointed at me, saying, "Yes, and we have here right now in our midst another writer, typical of the giants of letters that Minnesota produces. Stand up, Freddie, and let them see how big you really are."

I felt small for a moment. I could feel my face turn beet red.

Russell Fridley, sitting next to me, nudged me and told me to stand up. So I stood up.

Hubert laughed and said, "See? That's what I mean about a real Viking giant."

Many people complained that Hubert harangued too much in his talks, that he came on too strong, strident, didn't vary his attack enough, didn't speak softly at times. It was true that he was always in great high dudgeon about one problem or another.

But I heard another Hubert Humphrey the time he gave the main address at a national convention of historical society directors and historians in St. Paul. He'd asked that questions historians might be interested in be given him beforehand. Patiently, quietly, with wit and humor, and with a humor that was often directed at himself, at his own expense, he told about his visit to Chairman Khruschev in Moscow, his relations with President Lyndon Johnson, and the like. It was all done in an off-the-cuff conversational tone. I'd never heard him talk to better effect in my life. In fact, I'd never heard its equal anywhere. Before those hard-eyed historians he was open, frank, confessional. The audience began by being very silent and wound up laughing with enjoyment. It was a masterpiece of an evening.

Hubert had a monolithic intellect. He was very brilliant, with high peaks in politics and history. Some of us who knew him in the beginning used to lament a little that he didn't read enough outside his field, in fiction and poetry; that he didn't look into philosophy or astronomy or general science enough. When I first visited his house I was shocked to see how few books he had in his library. I've often wondered if his being color blind didn't have something to do with it, that he wasn't interested in those lively extra tones of life.

We all liked Muriel but some of Hubert's friends were heard to say they wished she could have been more of an intellectual helpmate for him. It was too bad, one old friend of his said, that Hubert hadn't married a rich cultural woman. In the long run though,

Muriel was just right for him. She kept his feet on the ground. He was a high flyer and had a tendency to forget he was only mortal.

Hubert was a man of endless energy. He was so full of energy that he remained boyish all his life. Even up to the very last he still had the air of a man who was running for office for the first time. He never got sick of politicking, as he called it. Myself, I got sick of saying the same thing the second time around. His ability to put fire and steam into an old subject was utterly out of my understanding. I'd have gone wild in a month if I'd had to give the same talk over and over again. I think it was the teacher in him, and his love for people, and his full-hearted concern for their destiny, that gave him the ability to repeat his lectures and talks and harangues ad infinitum. For me it would have been ad nauseam. But that was Hubert.

We're going to miss Hubert in the years to come. We already missed having a great president in him.

When he walked into a room it was like an extra current had been turned on. The lights in the room were suddenly brighter, the smiles were wider, and suddenly you were in glory land with Hubert.

He was a man of tremendous internal drive. Never did I see him in a down mood.

He was a great man to know.

May 31, 1978
At Roundwind

Ninety Is Enough
Portrait of My Father

MY FATHER WAS BORN IN THE SMALL VILLAGE OF TZUM, near Franeker, Friesland, in the Netherlands, March 31, 1886. He was baptized Feike Feikes Feikema VI, though he later was known as Frank Feikema.

The first Feike back in the 1750's had been a man of property, owning a big farm called Groot Lankum near Franeker, but he'd lost it due to a pestilence which wiped out his herd of Frisian-Holstein cattle. The once proud Feikemas fell into the labor market.

Feike V, my grampa, still had some of that old pride left in him. He refused to be a laborer, and instead sailed before the mast. He talked a lovely Frisian girl named Ytje Andringa, who came from a rich family, into eloping with him. When she was disinherited for doing so, Grampa Feike V decided he had enough of the Old Country, and with his wife and his just-born son, my father, left for the United States.

Several years ago, when I visited Tzum, I discovered that Grampa's house had been razed, along with others, and had become part of the property owned by an old people's home. I did find my father's name registered in the *Doop Boek* (birth book) in the beautiful old Tzum church and saw my grandfather's signature. I saw the font where my father was baptized. I tried to imagine what that baby might have looked like before it was whisked off to America.

When Grampa landed at Ellis Island, the immigration officer had trouble pronouncing his name, Feike F. Feikema. Finally the officer told Grampa that he'd better have at least a first name people could pronounce. He asked Grampa what town he came from, and when Grampa answered, first Frjentsjer, the Frisian version, and then Franeker, the Dutch version, the man said, "We'll put you down as Frank and whatever that last name of yours is." So Frank it was after that, and in time my father was called Frank too. That was a strange naming; the Frisians and the Franks had been enemies for centuries. Actually Frederick would have been a better translation. Frederick and Feike come from the same Indo-European root of *pri-tu* meaning "love, free, friend." And *ma* means "man of" or "son of."

Grampa and wife and child first headed for Orange City, Iowa, a Dutch settlement. Restless, still full of pride, Grampa next moved the family to Grand Rapids, Michigan, also a Dutch settlement and where some relatives of his wife lived; then to Perkins Corner, Iowa, where he farmed a quarter section; then to Lebanon, Missouri where he worked on a railroad; then to Doon, in Northwest Iowa, where he became a stone mason; then to what later became known as the Bad Lands of South Dakota; and finally to Doon again, where he built storm cellars and cement block houses and worked part time on the railroad as a section hand in the wintertime. Five more children were born to Grampa and Gramma during all that wandering, Kathryn, Jennie, Nick, Abben, and Gertrude. All were raised as Americans, not as Frisians or Hollanders. Grampa swore when he landed in America that he would never speak either Frisian or Dutch again, but only what he called "American." He made only one exception and that was to speak Frisian to his mother, my great-grandmother, who came to America shortly after he did and lived in Sioux Center, Iowa. My memory of Grampa is that he spoke good English, with no trace of a foreign accent. Frisians are related to the Angles and Saxons and have little trouble learning to speak English.

Shortly after Gertrude was born, Gramma Ytje died and the family was broken up. My father was farmed out to various American families living out in the country, the Pohlmans, the Harmings, the Reynolds, all of them originally coming from New England by way of the Western Reserve. Aunt Kathryn went to live with a wealthy family in town named Holmes. Thus at a very early age my father was taken out of school and such learning as he had soon vanished. It had also become apparent that he had some trouble learning in school, unlike Aunt Kathryn who was very good at it. He was good at figures but never letters. When he signed his name he had to stop and think each time he wrote a letter, as though he had trouble remembering their right order, which later on suggested to me that he may very well have had some form of dyslexia.

In the 1890s people got around by horseback or by horse and buggy. There still were many wild prairies left, especially along the rivers and where it was hilly. My father told me that he remembered riding a horse once for some ten miles without hitting a fence. Some homes were still being built of sod. There were no groves or trees about except along the rivers. There were of course no radios or telephones. There was a local newspaper, *The Doon Press*, but gossip moved slowly from home to home. And moving slowly, it was thoroughly digested, until various kinds of usable wisdom emerged.

Pa soon found out that he had a good ear for music and learned to play the harmonica, the accordion, and the fiddle. Presently he was in demand to play at as well as call square dances. The church he went to, the Congregational, didn't frown on dancing or singing. He also developed into a pretty fair country baseball pitcher.

He apparently was a doughty fellow. Once he accidentally jabbed a hayfork into his knee in the dead of winter. He was a long ways from the yard at the time but had the presence of mind to first make a tourniquet with his handkerchief before jerking the hayfork out of the bone. On another occasion, while shingling the cupola on the locally famous Reynolds round barn, the cleat on which his foot rested gave way, and he began sliding. He fell off the cupola and hit the main roof. Despite desperate clawing and scratching, he kept on sliding. When he knew there was no way of stopping the slide, he figured out where the fresh cow manure pile lay below and, deliberately rolling himself over and over as he slid, managed to aim himself for it. He shot out over the edge of the roof, and miracle of miracles, landed in six feet of loose green slush. The cupola was seventy feet above the ground. He came out of it covered with manure but otherwise "without a scratch."

Pa met my mother, Alice Van Engen, tall and golden blond, when he was twenty-three. There is no evidence that he had a girl friend before he met her, though I did hear from some old timers that the girls of his day considered him a catch. He was handsome with black hair, light gray piercing eyes, and a powerful six-foot-four frame. He liked to say that he was just as tall as Abraham Lincoln. He had fair skin and always had a sweet smell about him. Even when he sweat he had a good manly aroma about him. He danced with girls but didn't date them. He met my mother at her cousins' house on a farm near Doon. She'd had a sad romance with a fellow in Orange City, Iowa (my mother wouldn't let him kiss her much and the fellow, not being able to wait, knocked up the hired girl where he worked), and her father, my grampa Frederick Van Engen, sent her to her Van Engen cousins near Doon to get over it. While she was there, Pa happened to drive onto the Van Engen yard and the two fell for each other. From what my mother told me, and from what Pa has said, they were innocents, virgins, when they got married. My father often remarked to us boys, as though to instruct us, "When I got married I could look any woman in the world in the eye. And I still can."

Ma was devoutly religious, though not of the fanatic kind. She was gentle, quietly determined, and very bright. (I go into all this in great detail in my novel *Green Earth*, which is in part autobiographical.) She quietly got Pa to leave his church and to join hers, the Dutch Christian Reformed Church. She also persuaded him to quit playing and calling at square dances, though she didn't mind if he played his jolly tunes on the harmonica and the accordion at home. She herself was highly musical and they often played together, he on harmonica and she on the parlor organ. Sometimes she sang (she was a good soprano) while he played. She also urged him to quit playing baseball, "a little boy's game," but that he wouldn't do. He no longer played for the town team but did play for the church team. I remember only two arguments or tiffs between the two, and one of them had to do with baseball. It was the Fourth of July and Doon was playing Sioux Center at a church picnic. Pa was to play third base. Ma wanted him to listen to a famous Navajo missionary instead. Ma worked on him all the way to the picnic grove and all Pa did was smile his sideways smile. When they got there, Ma discovered the missionary had moved his talk up an hour so he could watch the game. Pa would never admit it but I think he knew that the missionary loved baseball.

Pa and Ma got married January 22, 1911. They had only a couple hundred dollars to begin farming and only a few possessions. They bought a team of horses (Pa already owned a wonderfully swift and willful trotter named Daise, a pretty roan), a cow, a heifer with calf, a few chickens, and a few pigs. They also bought a few implements at farm sales, a walking plow, a walking cultivator, a disk, a drag, a cornplanter. At the end of the first year they'd paid off all debts and bought more horses and cattle.

I was born January 6, 1912, during a fierce blizzard. It was 24° below. My grandmother, Jennie Van Engen, was there and she helped Ma have me while Pa was gone to fetch the doctor with a team and bobsled. When after a great struggle Pa and the doctor finally made it through the storm, I was already lustily bawling away. Earlier Pa had found a full bottle of whiskey in the haymow and he promptly asked Ma for permission to break it open and celebrate with the doctor.

My mother, who was death on drinking, reluctantly agreed. Later she took the bottle and put it in the bottom of her wardrobe. When my mother died in 1929 there actually was some whiskey left in that bottle. Uncle Hank, my mother's brother, gave her a slug of it to revive her for a time when she was dying of rheumatic fever.

My father insisted that I be named Frederick, and not either Feike or Frank. He had come to love my mother's father, Frederick Van Engen. Furthermore he was a little tired of all that Feike the Fifth and Feike the Sixth stuff. He stuck to his guns too when his father's brothers, my great uncles, drove great distances to protest my being named Frederick. "He is the Feike," the great uncles proclaimed, faces lived, "the stamhâlder, the son and heir, the seventh in a row since the first Feike!"

Pa's insistence on naming me Frederick helps explain why he didn't object when I changed my name from Frederick Feikema to Frederick Feikema Manfred in 1952. I'd found out from a linguist that Feike and Frederick had the same Indo-European root at about the same time that I had enough of having to spell out my name to long distance telephone operators as well as having to explain that as a Frisian-Saxon I really was about as Anglo-Saxon as anyone could be in the English-speaking world. Pa knew the problems of having a "funny name" in America.

My first memory of my father was the day he caught a ride to town with a neighbor and later in the afternoon, to our surprise, came rolling onto the yard driving a new car, a chain-drive Overland, beeping the bulb horn, scaring the dog into hiding under the corncrib, making the cattle bawl out in the barnyard, causing the horses out in the night yard to pop their tails, and chasing the chickens back into their coops. My mother appeared at the screen door to the kitchen, drying her hands in her green apron and wondering what all the racket was about. My father invited her to get in and he'd take us all for a spin around the section. My brother Edward and I quickly climbed in back, our usual seat in the carriage, breaths short for joy, eyes as wild as cock-eyed roosters. My mother got in very reluctantly. She didn't like "the automobile" as she always called it. Pa bugled the horn again and we were off. The sun was shining and all the neighbors' chickens were working the ditches for grasshoppers. When Pa blew the horn, the chickens sprayed in all directions. The front of the Overland went through them like the prow of a boat pushing through white water. When the ride was over, my mother got out of the car, not saying a word, and with a sick smile went directly back to her kitchen. Ma never did get to like "the automobile" and so long as she was alive she never permitted Pa to drive over 30 miles an hour. "Or I jump out."

Pa continued to surprise us when he came back from trips. One day he went to Sioux City with a shipment of hogs, taking the Great Northern from Doon. A day later he arrived home catching a ride with a neighbor. Eddie and I ran out to the gate to see who it was. When Pa stepped out of the car we didn't recognize him right away. Pa had bought himself a complete set of new clothes, a new gray overcoat with a black velvet collar, a new gray hat with a black band, a new gray suit, and a pair of black gloves. The face looked familiar but all those new clothes threw us off. Also this strange man with Pa's face didn't act like Pa. This man acted like a high monkey-monk from the city with fancy dude manners. He had a package with him which he carried into the kitchen and proceeded to open. It turned out to be a special dress, floor length, for my mother. It was when Pa took off his hat and bowed to Ma and then kissed her that I finally made out for sure who it really was.

One day I heard some coughing in the barn and when I looked I found Pa's favorite horse Daise down. I'd known he'd kept her in the barn that day for some reason, but I was shocked to see Daise lying on the floor. One never caught a horse down. I ran to get my father in the house. Pa was smoking his pipe, feet up on the reservoir of the stove. When I told him what I'd seen, Pa clapped out his pipe in the range, and hurried out to the barn. Pa took one look and knew the worst. He got down on his knees beside her and held her head.

After a while Daise coughed in his lap. That ignited Pa. He gently laid her head down in the straw and ran to the house to call the veterinarian. When my mother wondered a little about the cost of the long distance call, my father whirled on her and cried, "My God, woman, that's Daise that's sick! My Daise! You know, the pretty roan what's been with me all these years. Who even took me to Orange City to see you."

When he couldn't raise the vet, Pa asked Ma if she had some liniment around. She didn't. So next he asked her for the whiskey bottle lying in the bottom of her wardrobe. She gave it to him reluctantly. He ran to the barn with the whiskey to give Daise a slug of it. But Daise only coughed when he opened her lips and poured some into her mouth. The whiskey spilled out into the straw.

Daise was dead within the hour.

My father cried. I'd never before seen him cry and I was too petrified to move. I didn't want to see it but at the same time I couldn't move either. Pa dug a huge hole for Daise in the pasture and buried her. He refused to call the rendering plant.

I was about nine when my father awakened me in the middle of the night one March. He was full of tender concern, which surprised me. What was up? I soon learned. After I'd dressed we went to the hog barn. There he explained to me what he wanted. He had purebred Poland China sows, with papers, and they had one fault. Because of special breeding they often had difficulty giving birth. What was needed was a long slim arm to reach inside the sow to help the little piglets down the birth canal. Somewhat numb, and curiously also liking what I was doing, I helped most of those sows have their pigs that spring.

Later that year hog cholera hit. The vet came too late to give the little pigs serum and they all died. My father once again cried, and then retired to his favorite spot beside the kitchen stove, feet up on the reservoir, pipe clamped tight in his mouth. He refused to move. Ma didn't know what to do with him. Finally I took it upon myself to get out the old walking plow and open up a long deep furrow in the hog pasture and bury all the little pigs. They'd begun to stink and were covered with green flies. Gone was Pa's dream that by selling purebred hogs he could finally make a killing and then buy himself a farm. He and mother dreamed every spring that someday they'd own a farm and be independent. Both hated being renters. Pa with his brother Nick and his three sisters Kathryn and Jennie and Gertrude owned Grampa Feikema's cement block house in town, but that was not the same thing as owning a real farm.

It was about the same time that an investment man heard that Pa and Ma had managed over the years to build up a savings account of some fifteen hundred dollars. The man persuaded them to invest half of it, seven hundred fifty dollars, in the Northwest

Harness Company. It happened that Pa liked the Northwest harness for farm work. Pa thought them the sure thing. The man told Pa and Ma they were bound to double, if not triple, their money in a year's time. The company was new and was sure to grow. With fifteen hundred, possibly even two thousand two hundred fifty dollars, they would finally have enough to buy the farm they had their eye on. It would help make up for the loss of all those purebred Poland China pigs. But in 1922, during a recession, the Northwest Harness Company filed for bankruptcy.

That same summer Pa and Ma invested the remaining seven hundred fifty dollars in their savings account in a general store that a friend of theirs built in Lakewood, halfway between Doon and Rock Rapids, Iowa, for the convenience of nearby farmers. On stormy days, rain or snow, both Doon and Rock Rapids were pretty far away for quick shopping. Lakewood, unincorporated, had a grain elevator, a depot, a lumberyard, and a blacksmith. There were five houses.

One afternoon, no one knows how, a fire started in the storekeeper's house and then jumped across to the general store. There was no fire-fighting equipment in town. Ma learned about it via the country telephone when Central gave the alarm with a general ring. Pa with the whole family drove like mad to the final hill. When he saw how far along the fire was, he pulled up. Pa and Ma watched it all burn down from the hilltop. I remember staring down at the two great pillars of flames and smoke with a boy's deep sick feeling in my stomach. There went another seven hundred fifty dollars.

When there was nothing but ashes left, Pa turned the car around and drove home. All he said was, "Couldn't even get close enough to light my pipe with it."

At the Doon Christian Grammar School, which my mother

decided I should attend instead of the country public school, there were two boys much older than the rest of us. The law was that you had to go to school until you were sixteen. One noon when I went to the church horse barn where I kept my mare, Tip, I caught the two fellows tormenting her. They had climbed onto the rafter above her and with long sticks were jabbing her in the ass just under the tail, and laughing loudly when she bucked and eenked up in the air.

It happened that about a month before I'd complained to my father that these two fellows were bullies. My father listened a while and then gave me some father-son advice. "Look, what do you want me to do, take off work and go to school and punish those boys for you? Their parents would be in an uproar if I did that. No, son, that's a battle you've got to fight yourself. Even if they're much bigger than you, go after them. Let them know you're a fierce critter if they push in too far. Go after them even if you know you're going to lose. They'll remember your teeth the next time." He paused; then went on. "Course I don't ever want to hear that you started the fight. Or that you're a bully. Then you're going to have to deal with me. But otherwise, if you know you're in the right, fight!"

Seeing those two bozos tormenting my horse enraged me. I lost complete control of myself. I never once gave it a thought that both of them were twice as strong as I was. I grabbed Tip's bridle which was hanging on a nail behind her and went after them. They made one mistake. They dropped down off the rafter and, still laughing at the great joke of it all, started to run for the rear of the barn thinking to "escape" that way. But the rear door had been nailed shut and they couldn't get out. I had them cornered. Tip's bridle had a heavy breaker bit in it because she had too strong a mouth for me. The bit was a good inch thick, and heavy, and every time I came around with it over their backs as they tried to scrunch down as small as possible in the corner of the stall, they yelped twice as loud as Tip ever did. Finally an image of my mother popped into my head, and she asked, "Boy, boy, is this what I raised you to be? A killer? Alice's boy?" I let up. But I swear that if her image hadn't spoken up, I would have killed them. It's the only time in my life I ever thought of killing anyone.

My father was soon called before the church consistory. The minister told him what the problem was. His boy, Freddie Feikema, had beat up on two boys, members of the church, and what did he have to say about it. My father got to his feet and said he'd like to ask one question of each of the parents of the two boys.

He asked the first parent, "Nuh, and how old is your boy?"

"Well, yah, he is going on sixteen."

He asked the second parent, "And your boy?"

"Well, yah, Frank, you know, he's going on sixteen too."

Pa then turned to the minister. "Domeny, my boy is only ten years old. Why, even the horse they was tormenting is younger than them." And left.

I was in high school, going to Western Academy in Hull, Iowa, some seven miles away, when one weekend in late November, running all the way home, bursting into the kitchen, I found my father sitting beside the stove again, feet up on the reservoir. This time, instead of smoking his pipe, he was holding a hand over his nose. Something wild had happened. His nose was as purple as a plum and as big as an Idaho potato. There was still some blood on his upper lip.

Mother was ironing workshirts nearby. "Yes," she said, pointing her iron at Pa, "there sits a man who's now taken to jumping off windmills. Instead of just barns. And worse yet, there sits a man who won't go to see a doctor when he might be mortal hurt." My mother rarely indulged in irony, but when she did angels revolted in heaven.

I asked what had happened.

Pa didn't say a word.

Ma said, "Like I just said, he jumped off the windmill."

Pa finally said, voice nasal and gravelly, "Naw, not that. Like I said before, one of them rungs on the ladder broke and I fell off."

"You said you jumped the last ways."

"Well, yeh, after I saw I was gonna fall."

"You could have at least called the doctor." Ma went on to explain what Pa had done instead of going to the doctor. He'd whittled out two pieces of soft willow twigs, doped them with horse salve, then slowly stuck them up his broken nose and molded the nose into shape around the twigs.

I winced.

Pa saw my look. "Nah, you better get your yard duds on and do the chores. You still know what to do, don't you? Schooling still ain't chased that out of your head yet, has it?"

I hurried into my clothes. Without Pa, I'd have my hands full getting everything done on time, the feeding of the hogs and cattle and chickens and horses, milking and separating, feeding the calves. Eddie was a help but he was slow. But before I began, I had to know what had happened. I hurried down the hog pasture to the old wooden mill with its huge wooden fan. The fan was stuck; it was half-turned around, facing the wind when it should have been going with the wind. I climbed up the wooden ladder until I found the broken rungs just at the entrance to the platform on top. There were three of them. They'd become rotted at the nail holes and parts of the rungs were still caught in the three nails. I climbed down carefully, noting as I did so there were other near-rotted rungs. I next worked out where he'd fallen. The ground was frozen some two inches deep, and I found where his heels had hit and dug a hole some three inches deep through the layer of frost and the softer earth beneath. The next thing I saw was a gouge in the earth some fifteen feet farther along. There was blood in the gouge. It must have been the place where his nose had hit. I looked up at the mill platform above me and figured Pa must have dropped a good fifty feet.

I had trouble understanding it all, and was trying to imagine how it happened, when I heard some neighing behind me. Looking around, I saw Pa's team of grays, Pollie and Nell, still hitched to the cornfield fence. The wagon was half-full of picked corn. Pa was almost finished picking corn; there were still two rows left. When he came to the end of the field he must have noticed that the mill was stuck and had climbed up it to turn the head around.

Pa back at the house hadn't mentioned the horses and the wagon out in the field. It meant he'd really banged his head, so hard he'd forgotten that he'd been picking corn. I climbed the fence, untied the horses, and drove them home. The sun was just setting, shooting great strokes of amber across the rolling fields.

Later on I got Pa to tell me how it really happened. I had to know. Just as I'd guessed he'd decided to turn the mill head around before picking the last two rows of the year. The mill head had somehow gotten stuck. The windmill could be pumping water while he picked. Just as he took hold of the top rung into the opening of the platform, it broke in his hands. "I quick grabbed for the next one," he said. "But it too broke in my hands. I made one more grab for the next one, and when that broke, I knew I was gonna go. When I looked down, I saw how the old mill was all spraddled out as it went down and I knew that if I didn't jump outwards, I'd fall into those cross bars and really wreck myself. So I jumped for all I was worth. Then, as I fell, I knew that if I didn't do something special, I'd spill my guts all over the hog pasture. I then remembered how grasshoppers lit after they'd jumped, their legs all scissored up like so, so I pulled my feet up into a half-crouch. By that time I was hitting the earth. And by dab, if I didn't land like a grasshopper and then bounce ahead. I couldn't quite get my hands out ahead of me in time, so that's why my nose took such an awful wallop. It knocked me out for a little bit too."

I kept thinking that he could have broken a leg or a hip joint. But he never complained about any aching bones or joints.

"Just that fetchsticking nose, which I had to remodel to look a little like I use to."

It was also about that time that Pa realized he was losing me. As long as I was a little boy I'm sure he always believed I'd become his right hand man on the farm. He rejoiced in the way I caught on how to do things: milking, driving horses, starting engines on cold mornings. But as the weeks and years went by it became pretty obvious that I was going to be a lover of books. Whenever we went to visit the neighbors, I always checked the neighbors' parlor first to see if they had any books before I went outside to play with their children under the trees.

"You've always either got your head in a book or in a cloud," Pa would say. "And when you walk across the yard, even with you staring down at the ground, you don't see what's underfoot. Pick up that loose piece of butcher paper there and put it somewhere. There's nothing so unsightly as a littered yard. Pick up, pick up, pick up."

Yet in a curious way, ambivalent, he gloried in my ability to read important documents for him. I started high school at the age of twelve, far too young really, but for his boy he thought it nothing unusual. When I told him stories about happenings at the academy, he'd follow my telling with a high light in his gray eyes, lips imitating my lip movement, waiting for the punch line so he could burst out laughing.

Except for one year, when I ran the seven and a half miles to and from school every day, he always took time off from work and brought me to school on Monday mornings. When it was raining he took the horse and buggy and when it was dry he took the old Buick.

In 1928, right after I'd graduated from the academy, we began to get little signals that Ma wasn't feeling too well. She spoke of fainting spells, of her heart beating funny. None of us children (by this time Mother had six sons and no daughters) believed that it was serious. Fathers and mothers just never died. They were always there. Just like God was always there.

But Pa took it seriously. They tried various doctors. By the time Ma arrived at the doctor's office she usually looked like she was in the bloom of health. She'd had a rest on the way over. Finally one doctor said it was her teeth and told her to have them all pulled. It was while she was having her lowers removed that she fainted dead away. It took some desperate action on the part of the dentist, Dr. Maloney, to get her back. From that day on she began to go downhill.

When she died on April 19, 1929, my father took it hard. (I was home at the time; my mother had asked me not to start college until I was eighteen.) Pa looked like a tall cottonwood with the upper branches blasted white by lightning. He was one of those who'd turned gray early, but on her death he rapidly turned white. We had no housekeeper, couldn't get one in those days, and the days were dark in that country farmhouse east of the Doon water tower. Pa never struck us, or cursed us, just went about in white-haired smoldering sorrow. But he kept us neat. He did most of the housework (cooking, washing clothes, ironing) plus doing his share of the yard work. He got us to church in time on Sundays. When company dropped by, he was polite, and set out the coffee and cake just as Ma would have done it.

In the middle of that dark sorrowing time, my brother Ed almost got killed. It was in November and very cold. The month before there'd been a powerful south wind for several days, sometimes almost eighty miles an hour, and it had ripped a lot of corn ears from the stalks, at least a good third of them. With Pa up on the cornpicking machine, Ed and I followed him, bent over as we ran along picking up the fallen ears and tossing them into the open section of a small elevator in the back of the machine. That running and gathering on the run just about killed us.

Pa felt sorry for us and gave us a lot of rests at the end of the field. Once we stopped on the far side of the north seventy. We were about a half mile from the house.

Our breaths caught, Pa climbed back up on the machine. He unloosened the lines to the five horses and shook them, saying, "Giddap. Time to get going again."

The horses didn't move. The bitter north wind was on their tail and they had it cozy for the moment.

Again Pa called out his resonant, "Giddap!"

Still they didn't move.

"Ed, pick up a clod there and toss it onto Old Nell's tail. That'll wake her up." Nell was in the lead team and was the most dependable horse we had.

Ed picked up a clod and deftly hit Nell in the tail with it. She didn't even switch her tail at it.

"By gorry now," Pa exclaimed. "Ed, pick up another clod, this time a big one, and let her have it harder."

Ed had to kick around in the frozen ground to find a clod. Finally he found one in front of the snout of the cornpicker. He chunked the big frozen clod hard on Nell's tail. That woke her up, and she leaned into her traces. The other four horses woke up then too.

The picker was always heavy-ended on the snout or left side, and the paired snouts swung left and grabbed Ed's right leg. He didn't have a chance to get out of the way in time. The snapping rollers began to chew into his leg. Ed was too startled to cry out.

Pa saw it all in a glance, and he hauled back on all five lines with all his might and let go with a great chilling, "WHOA!" His voice, always powerful, so pierced the consciousness of those five horses they all froze in their tracks.

Holding tight onto the lines, Pa barked, "Fred, unhitch those horses one at a time. Queen first, since she's the friskiest. And let's hope she don't smell the blood." He leaned back to shut off the machine.

I unhitched Queen and Pa let go of her line. I led her to the fence and tied her to it. Then I peeled off the rest of the four horses, with Pa all the while sitting up on the picker seat eyes alert for the least motion in the machine. If those snapping rollers made one more revolution Ed's leg was gone. Ed meanwhile stood absolutely still, as though a wrestler had him by the leg and the best policy was just to stand still.

The moment I started to lead the last horse away, Pa scrambled down off the machine and had a look at Ed's leg. I joined him. The snapping rollers had just begun to grind into the bone about a half foot above the ankle.

"Ed, Ed," was all Pa said; and then, all business, he told me what wrenches to get from the toolbox on the back of the picker. Working carefully, silently, Pa and I managed to take off enough nuts to loosen the snapping rollers and open up the metal snout a little. Ed stood silent above, an occasional tear dropping off his wind-red cheeks and falling on our hands. Finally, thinking he had enough room, Pa began to extricate the mashed leg. I got to my feet and held Ed up.

When we finally got the leg out, we discovered that Ed could still stand on it. And it was then, everything finally safe, that Pa let go. He simply bowed over and cried, grinding his teeth.

The crying lasted about thirty seconds. Then, having had enough of that, Pa got hold of himself and half-carrying Ed helped him home and took him to the doctor. It took several months for Ed's leg to heal.

The incident added gloom to the household.

Worse yet, Pa got undulant fever that winter. He'd be his usual self for about an hour in the morning, and then was done for the day and had to go to bed. That left a lot of the yard work in my hands. In a way it was lucky it was winter; there was no field work to do.

When pigging time came around, Pa called me into the bedroom. "Son, according to my calendar, those sows will be coming in any day. Now you know what I've been doing the last couple of years. Trading young boars with a fellow from Edgerton, Minnesota, so's not to get inbreeding."

"I know," I said.

"Well, now when those pigs start coming in, I want you to watch for the peppiest and orneriest little boar pig in each litter. Make a mark in your mind about him. Do that with each litter. And when all the pigs are in, we'll trade our peppiest little boar for a peppy boar from that fellow in Edgerton. That little boar will be the one to wake up first after he's born, be the first to crawl between his mother's legs to get to titty, be so ornery about it he'll want all those tits to himself until he's had enough. You know, make a real hog of himself."

I wasn't sure I liked hearing all that.

"There may be one or two others that'll be just about as good, and if our first one dies, they'll make pretty good replacements."

"Yes, Pa."

"The rest of the males we'll nut. They won't be much good for anything but fattening."

"How about the gilts, must I watch them too to see which ones will make good breeding stock?"

"Naw. Cripes, where've you been raised? Naw, most all of them will make good sows. And you know, that's a funny thing. Let's say we get a hundred little pigs. About fifty-four of them will be males, and forty-six females. Some ten of those males will be stumperts, peewees, and will die no matter what you do for them. And there will be at the most only two females that'll die. All the rest of the females will make good breeding stock. All of them. Sometimes of those forty-four that are left I have a hard time picking the twenty I want to keep for breeding sows next year."

A thought shot through my head. "Is that true of human beings too, Pa? Where only one or two of the men are any good and the rest peewees? And where most of the women are good?"

A big smile grew sideways across Pa's grizzled chin. "I wouldn't want to say. Besides, I dassent ask around of my friends."

Some twenty years later I happened to tell this story to Dr. Starke Hathaway, psychologist at the University of Minnesota, the man who invented the Minnesota Multi-phasic Personality Inventory test. He let out a hoot and started to laugh. "Why, there's a fellow down at Indiana University who's been making a survey of human beings on that very subject. A guy by the name of Alfred C. Kinsey."

That summer, undulant fever gone, Pa managed to get a housekeeper named Hattie. She had eight daughters and one son. Three of the youngest daughters began living with us. All the rest were married. With all that femininity around us, things changed drastically in our home.

Later Pa married Hattie. They didn't always get along, which was a grief to Pa, since he hated all dissension. He'd only had two disagreements with our own mother, mentioned above, and he didn't know how to handle it. But as time went on, as he put it, "We managed to bang it out together until we got along better."

In the fall of 1935, a year after I'd graduated from college, I hitchhiked home to visit my father. I still didn't have a steady job. I helped him get out the last of the corn and then went over to a neighbor to help him finish picking his corn by hand. It had been a bad year for farmers. The corn was mostly nubbins, short stubby ears, hard to jerk out of the husk, and the pay was poor.

When there were no more odd jobs to do, I found myself at loose ends. I loved my father and my five brothers and liked living with them again for a while. But it was uneasy living under the same roof with a stepmother who quarreled with my father a lot and who in addition considered me a college bum because I didn't actively seek a teaching job, for which I was qualified with a Life Certificate from the state of Michigan. But what I'd seen of practice teaching, and of teachers, I knew it wasn't for me, especially if I wanted to write.

Then my stepmother got an idea. Why didn't we go to Los Angeles and visit two of her daughters. As long as I didn't have anything to do, I could drive for them. Pa had just traded in the old Chevy for a new Dodge so we could ride in style. After some talk it was agreed that we'd go. We took with us a farm boy named Bill DeBoer who wanted to try his luck milking cows in Artesia near Los Angeles.

We started very early one morning from Doon, in the northwest corner of Iowa, and headed down 75 past Sioux City, and at Freeman, Nebraska, picked up Highway 30 and headed west across Nebraska. We drove steadily all day. It got dark while we were still

in Nebraska. And it was around ten when we got a cabin in Chey-
enne. There were no motels in those days. All day long all we'd
seen was flat land, sometimes gently rolling land, not unlike the
land around Doon. During those hours when we drove in darkness,
the gathering hills of Wyoming couldn't be made out.

We woke to a deep fog in the morning. Visibility was almost
zero. We had breakfast, and then slowly, lights on, we started out.
As usual I drove, with the farm boy Bill sitting next to me in front,
with Pa and Hattie in back, Pa sitting on the right side. From the
sound of the motor I could tell after a while we were climbing. But
from what we could see, a few feet on either side of us, and for all
we knew, we were still traveling across flat land.

We came around a slow curve, going left, when abruptly the
fog lifted, and below us on the right lay a vast long valley. We were
traveling along the top of a mountain. Pa popped bolt upright on
his side, staring down at the valley. He exclaimed in Frisian, his
mother tongue, "Gotske, hwet gatten!" He pronounced the last
two words as, "Hwat gawten!" It means in English, "God, what
holes!" I hadn't heard him speak Frisian for years. What with
his father dead and most of his uncles gone, he rarely spoke it any
more. Then, as the road dipped down and the mountain side rose
on our left, he said, "Why, these things (the mountains) are upside-
down holes!"

I've laughed about that many times. For a true expression of
awe I've never heard it beat. It could have been Jim Bridger saying
it the first time he saw the mountains.

It was on that same trip that Pa stunned me with his talent for
music. One evening as Hattie and her two daughters were having
a good time gossiping, Pa said to me, "Ain't there anything going
on in this town that you and I could see?" I told him that I thought
maybe there was and looked through the amusement section of the

Los Angeles Times. I spotted a little story about the operetta *The Countess Maritza* being given in a theatre downtown.

"Hey," Pa said, "I'd like to see that. We had an opery house in old Doon once and I saw a good one there."

We got there early and took one of the cheaper seats. I told Pa how I and my friends in college used to get cheap seats and then watched to see what seats weren't sold up front and, after the first intermission, stole down and took them. Pa thought that a great idea.

We never got around to it. A few minutes into the singing, I heard a sound next to me. I looked. It was my father, crying. Tears were streaming down his cheeks, he thought the lyrics so beautiful. We didn't get up during either intermission. Afterwards, as I drove home, he still didn't say anything. He was too choked up with all the lovely music. When we got to the house the first thing he did was to ask his stepdaughter if she had a harmonica or an accordion in the house. She had an accordion, which her boy friend owned. Pa got it out and then, before my astonished eyes, proceeded to play most of the operetta *The Countess Maritza* back from memory.

My passionate strong-willed father was basically a musician who'd never had a chance to develop his talent.

A couple of years later Hattie decided she wanted to see her California daughters again. But she was puzzled as to how they'd make it safely without a driver to read maps.

Pa said, "Oh, well, if that's where you want to go I'll get you there. We don't need any map readers."

Sure enough, Pa talked her into going without a map reader. They took the exact same route that I drove. Pa remembered all the corners where you had to turn. Hattie told me afterwards that she was as astonished as anyone when Pa pulled up in front of her daughter's door without once having to ask for directions. His head was full of landscapes, one flowing into another.

Restless, Pa quit farming in the fall of 1935 and ran a filling station at Perkins Corner, Iowa, for a year in 1936. That wasn't the right thing for him either, so he quit that and came back to Doon and ran a dairy for a few years. It still wasn't right, so he sold the dairy and ran a cafe in Sibley, Iowa. That too turned sour on him and he took up carpentering. It developed that he was an excellent woodworker.

It was about that time that I came down with tuberculosis. I took the rest cure at the Glen Lake Sanatorium near Minneapolis. Pa came to see me at least once a month. While some of my other relatives might come to gloat over me, thinking, as I lay in my white bed, that's what Fred got for dreaming of becoming a big shot, a writer, Pa sat quietly by. All I can remember of those visits of his are four words, "Hello, son," and, "Good-bye, son." In between-times he tried to smile. Several times he'd take my hand and hold it a while. He was so gentle about it that at the time I completely forgot the few lickings he'd given me.

I didn't see much of him after I left the sanatorium. I got married and had part-time jobs and starting writing books. My wife Maryanna was never sure she liked him. She spoke of the piercing quality of his light-gray eyes. The way he looked at women always made her feel uncomfortable.

When I did see him he was always curious about my work. He couldn't read my books, but he was always interested to know about their success. He carried newspaper clippings about them in his pocket book.

When the Second World War came along, Pa heard the Navy needed woodworkers in California. The pay was very good, better than anything offered for carpenter work in Sibley, Iowa. He decided to give it a try and got a job doing the woodwork in the captain's cabin in Liberty ships. Hattie soon followed with the children and Pa became a Californian.

I wasn't there when Hattie died. From what my brothers John and Abben, who'd also gone to live in California, told me, it was pretty rough on him. He didn't like living alone. His stepchildren, all of Hattie's eight girls and their children, had come to love him as their own father and spent a lot of time visiting him. But at night when he went to bed he was still alone.

One day his milkman told him, "Frank, it ain't good for you to live alone like this. I can see it's getting you down."

"That's old news," Pa said.

"Tell you, Frank. I got a lady on my route who lost her sidekick a year ago and she too mopes around feeling sorry for herself. Why don't I have you two come over for dinner next Sunday so you can look each other over."

"Nah, it's too late."

"When you're both so lonesome? I tell you, you two were made for each other. I'll expect you next Sunday for dinner. Two bells."

"I'll think about it."

So the two met, Pa and Beatrice, in the milkman's house for dinner. And after the dinner they went their separate ways.

Pa thought about it for a week, then called Beatrice up and asked if he could come over for a cup of coffee the next Sunday. She thought it a fine idea.

She had him sit at her kitchen table while she set out the coffee and cake. They talked about the weather and how California was a fine place for people with old bones.

Pa had picked up his cup of coffee, and was about to take a sip, when he set the cup down again. "Say, Bea, before we go any further, you got to agree to one thing. It's something we better get straight right from the start."

"What's that, Frank?"

Pa had found out that she was Catholic and what he was about to ask her was a tough thing. He was still Christian Reformed (the word Dutch had been dropped by his church by then). "Well, Bea, you got to agree to join my church or it's all over between us."

Bea was startled, but she had come to like Pa's forthrightness. Furthermore, as Beatrice Roxanna Torrey before she got married to her Catholic husband, she'd originally been a Protestant in Haverhill, Massachusetts. "All right, Frank. If that's what you want, that's what it'll be."

So in a strange way my father's life had come full circle. He'd started out as a young boy living with Protestants who'd originally come from New England and he was now going to marry a Protestant who'd come from there.

One of my brothers was a little shocked that Pa wanted to get married again. The brother called me long distance.

"But, Fred, he's been married twice before. He should start thinking about the next life. Why should he want to get married again at his age? He's seventy-one. And then too, this Bea is so much younger than him. Much younger."

"So what? If they love each other that's all that counts. Age has nothing to do with it. She might just pep him up enough to give him another twenty years of life. No, I'm all for it."

"But she smokes cigarettes! It's funny that Pa would want to tolerate that. You know how he always was about bobbed hair women smoking in public. He's acting silly in his old age."

"Maybe he loves her."

They did love each other. Whenever we visited them and were

about to take them out to dinner, we could never get them to sit separate, whether it was riding over in the car or at the table. Several times we tried to get one of my brothers to sit between them but that didn't work.

"Hyar, not on your life," Pa would exclaim. "Bea sits with me or we don't go out."

Once we did manage to get him in the front seat and Bea in the back. All the way over to the steakhouse she leaned forward and put her hand on his shoulder while he reached back with a hand and placed it on hers.

I stayed with them many times. Lying on the couch which had been opened out to make a bed for me, I used to listen to them talk in their bedroom, door open. They had a light teasing game going at all times. Nothing rough, or mean. Tender. About whose turn it was to get up and make the coffee. Both loved that coffee spout. About who had the most pep. Both bragged to beat the band about that. About who scratched the worst with their toenails during sleep. It made me cry listening to them. It was the happiest chatter I'd ever heard between two people, especially between a man and a woman.

Bea once confessed to me, "Fred, that father of yours is almost too much for me. Heh. Such a sweet pest. But I wouldn't want to have him any different."

One day Pa came to me with a request. "Fred, one of these days it'll be time for me to go on. As well as for Bea."

"Naturally, Pa."

"You're my oldest son and so I'm telling you. You know how I loved your mother Alice. She was a fine woman. A good mother to all you boys. And you know how I got along with Hattie. But, Fred, I tell you, Bea is the best yet. She surely is a good woman. I'm really sweet on her and I want to be buried with her. And she wants that too. She says I'm her best man. I hope that's all right with you."

"Pa, I can't legislate your love affairs. We'll do what you ask of us."

Everybody had expected Pa to go first, he was so much older, twenty years. In fact when Pa and Bea first got married some of her friends thought it terribly unfair to Bea. She'd only have him a couple of years and then she'd once more be alone. She'd be much better off marrying someone her own age.

But Bea died first, of lung cancer. She'd never given up her smoking, especially not since Pa always enjoyed his pipe.

My youngest brother Henry saw Bea during her last days. "It was something to see when Pa went to visit her in the hospital. She'd be almost comatose until we'd enter her room. Then, the moment she'd hear Pa's voice, she'd light all up again. And when he said good-bye, he'd pick her up, she was so shrunken by then, and give her a hug and a kiss. It shook me up something terrible to watch that."

Once again at eighty-eight he was alone. It was decided by my two California brothers, John and Abben, that he should be moved to a home for the elderly. He was given a good room, had his favorite chair and television set, his box of pictures and other mementos.

He took it hard for a while. Then, picking up what he would call his gumption, he decided to learn to read. It was about time. He'd watch programs on public television showing the text of certain books and plays. By following the words shown with the voice reading them he managed to build up a reading vocabulary.

John learned about it one day when he dropped by to ask if Pa had got any mail he wanted read to him.

"Yeh, I got mail all right. A letter from Fred."

"Well, here, let me read it to you."

"I already read it."

"What?"

With a smile. "Yeh, I learned to read a little." Then Pa explained how he'd done it.

I visited him in October of 1976. He was eighty-nine. I was astonished to see how sharp his mind was. His memory of the old days was very keen. I didn't tell him at the time that I was writing *Green Earth*, a novel about our family, about his and my mother's life before I was born, all the way to her death when I was seventeen. I needed to know some details about the time when our new Reo threw a piston. I first told him what I remembered. He shook his head. "That ain't the way it went." Then he proceeded to go into such exact detail that I knew right away that his version was right and mine was slightly off. But I kept my version in the novel; it made for a better story.

The second day I was there visiting him, someone asked me a question about something I'd talked about when I'd first arrived. When I finished, Pa gave me a raised brow look. "That ain't the way you told it yesterday." I was stunned. He not only could remember things accurately from the distant past, but he could remember in detail what had happened the day before.

His hearing remained keen until the very end. He had good eyes and used glasses only for what he called close work. He had a little trouble walking the last couple of years because a young doctor had removed a thick callus from his foot. The callus should have been soaked off. When the scar finally healed he got around quite well again and walked as straight as ever. He prided himself in walking straight even though he was very tall. Three of his sons grew to be taller than his six foot four. I became six nine, Edward John became six eight, and Floyd became six six. Henry, the youngest, at six four became as tall as Pa. The other two, John and Abben, weren't quite as tall. He got after every one of us to stand straight and walk straight. He had to get after me the most because I had trouble with six-foot-eight doorways.

The last time I saw him I noticed how steady his long fingers were.

Then the next August, 1976, he'd had enough. He told my brother John that he was ready to go. There was nothing more for him to do. He'd pretty much done it all. There was nobody around he knew any more.

John tried to talk him out of the mood. "But you got us. And then there's all your grandchildren and great grandchildren."

"You boys are great, of course. But you're related to me and that ain't the same as being friends. We didn't choose each other."

Several times he was heard to say strange things. One of them was, "Where is everybody? Nobody around I can talk old times with any more. When I start telling my children about that baseball game at Alvord, where they tagged that guy out at home plate with a potato, they say, 'But Pa, you told us that yesterday already.' Well, I want to talk to somebody who'd like to hear that story again because they saw it too. Because it was a funny thing to see."

Again and again John would try to divert his attention to all his wonderful grandchildren, who loved him.

Pa hardly heard him. "Everybody in my bunch is gone. And if there is one left, he won't know from nothing no more. No, I've outlived all other memories but my own. Kids my own age, kids ten years younger, kids twenty years younger, are all gone. Why, I've even outlived my young wife and her bunch, so I can't talk about even their old stories. I'm forsaken, that's what I am. Left behind."

The nurses would sometimes try to pep him up. It didn't help much. Not even the nurse he sometimes had an eye for could get him out of his mood.

"No, I think I'll go now," he said. "I've had just about everything earth has to offer. I've finished all my jobs. I miss Bea. I want to go jolly her up." He'd shake his hoary old head on which the white hair had become so old it'd turned yellow. "Bea surely was a good wife. We always had a joke going. She was neat too, with the house, with her body. That's important for a woman to do. She always smelled like cinnamon and wild roses."

"Oh, c'mon now, Pa, there's a lot left yet for you to do."

"For the first time I feel as old on the inside as I look on the outside. Ninety is enough. Be good to my grandchildren. Maybe they can do it. Live forever."

Over the next month his vital signs slowly went down. His doctor put him under an oxygen tent.

"What's that thing doing here? I want to go. Get it out of here."

It was removed. His doctor next gave him heavier doses of vitamin pills and had special foods served him.

"I don't want those things. I liked the old grub."

Then on the morning of September 30th, 1976, Pa rang for the nurse. He had to go to the bathroom and he'd promised that if he got out of bed he'd always call the nurse. He refused to use a urinal. The nurse helped him to the bathroom and back to his bed.

Pa sat down on the edge of his bed. With a little smile he said, "Well. I feel pretty good. Now I'm ready for a good breakfast."

"I'll get it for you," the nurse said.

Pa lay down then to wait for the breakfast. The moment his head touched the pillow he was gone.

We buried him with Bea. In California.

July, 1978
At Roundwind

Sinclair Lewis

A Portrait

ANGELA IS TWENTY-TWO WAS IN TOWN (Minneapolis) with Red
Lewis starring in his own play. I bought a ticket to see it, and afterwards, when a friend of mine who was a *Time* reporter asked me to
go along with him to interview Sinclair, I also got a brief close-up of
him for the first time — the brief close-up being the length of time it
took Red to poke his lean hawk's head around the corner of the door
to say no, he was too busy seeing friends and relatives down from
his home town, Sauk Centre. The *Time* man was a considerate
fellow, and I was timid, so we backed away and had ourselves a
beer and ham-on-rye instead at the old Stockholm Cafe.

My next contact with him came when he was conducting a
writing class at the University of Minnesota in the fall quarter of
1942. At the time I didn't believe anyone could teach another to
write, but I did think that a successful writer could give a few
pointers on how to place a completed manuscript. I wanted Red
to read and to advise me on one of my three as yet unpublished
novels, and I asked the head of the English department, the poet
and critic Joseph Warren Beach, to intercede for me. The answer
I got came in the form of a letter, as follows:

Minneapolis
November 22, 1942

Dear Mr. Feikema:

I'm really sorry, but between the MSS I already have to
read for my students, and the desperate final work on my new

novel, which must be finished by Christmas, it would be quite impossible for me to read your novel.

Sincerely yours,
Sinclair Lewis

Then in the summer of 1944, our lives touched again. This time it came in the form of a protest from him. It seems that he had swooped in on the Regional Writing Committee of the University of Minnesota to have a look at the list of names of those given writing fellowships the previous year. I had been given one, and when he came across the title of my first novel, *The Golden Bowl*, to be published that fall, he entered a lengthy and emphatic protest with the secretary, Helen Clapesattle. He said I just simply could not and should not use a title that Henry James had already used for one of his novels. This protest came to me through my publisher, Paul Hillestad at the Itasca Press in St. Paul, Minnesota. Paul and I considered it at some length, but we finally decided to keep it, despite the objection that seemed, to me at least, to come from Mount Olympus, since the forms for the book were already set and since this was already a shortened form of my first title, *The Golden Bowl Be Broken*. Paul argued that the book trade folk would call it *The Golden Bowl* anyway, and I was thinking that we should use the ironic comment of the dusted-out farmers themselves for the title.

Then in January, 1946, I got to spend a long weekend, really almost a week, with Lewis in his own home up at Duluth, in the company of my wife Maryanna and Ann Chidester, another Minnesota writer. Enough time had passed by then for him to get around to reading my first novel, *Golden Bowl*. From what he said later, I learned that he had liked *Bowl* very much, and that he had quietly sent it on to the American Academy of Arts and Letters fiction committee, which awarded me, along with Jean Stafford, one of the 1945 grants-in-aid for a thousand dollars.

My wife and I had just bought a place out in the country. What with the furnace still not in and only an old oil stove to heat one room, my wife and I decided that she and the baby should stay in town with Gramma while I stayed out alone to finish the final pages of my third novel, *This Is the Year*.

It was the evening of the fourteenth, and I was in the midst of making a lonesome bachelor's meal of fried potatoes, steak, onions, along with tea, when the phone rang. In the mixup and uproar of settling into the house it happened that the electric stove had been set near the old-style country wall phone, and so while I answered it I kept right on stirring the potatoes and watching the steak.

It was the operator at the Leamington Hotel. Making sure she had her man, she put me through to a room, and the next voice I heard was a man's, clear, quick, nervous, high-pitched.

"Mr. Feikema?" The man had the accent right, on the first syllable.

"Yes?"

"This is Sinclair Lewis speaking."

"Oh," I said — flatly, because I didn't think it possible.

"Mr. Feikema, I'm simply delighted to hear your voice. I've read your *Golden Bowl*, and I'd like to meet you. Are you coming into Minneapolis one of these days by any chance?"

"Why, yes, it just happens I am coming in tomorrow."

"Wonderful. Wonderful. Could you drop in and see me? I'll be free all afternoon."

"Yes, I could."

"Good. How about coming up to my rooms in the Leamington at, say, around four?"

"Sounds good to me."

"Wonderful." By the way his voice rose and fell I could tell that he was jumping around excitedly on the other end of the wire. "This is wonderful. A great pleasure. I've been looking forward to this. Really. I'm just simply delighted to hear your voice at last and that we'll meet."

"And I'm delighted." My voice was still flat, mostly because I still didn't think it possible that Sinclair Lewis was talking to me and was asking to see me. In fact, I was busy wondering if it couldn't possibly be one of my friends pulling my leg again.

We hung up. When I looked down, I found that my potatoes and steak and onions were burning.

I went in the next day and just for the heck of it took the precaution of buying his latest book, *Cass Timberlane*, and also one of my own, *Boy Almighty*. When I told the clerk, in boyish confidence, that I was buying *Cass* in the hope that I might get Red Lewis to autograph it, she shook her head and said he rarely did that for anyone any more. But I took the two books with me anyway.

I knocked on his door at precisely four. It was cold, and I remember that I was all bundled up in a big greatcoat and a high fur hat. The door opened and a pair of luminous gray-green eyes topped by thinning white hair looking up at me, looked up even though the head was tilted forward and down. Pale, almost imperceptible brows had climbed halfway up a high blond forehead.

"Mr. Lewis? I'm Feikema."

He exploded into action and seized my hand with both of his, excitedly, and said, "This is a pleasure. A real pleasure. Come in, come in. Here. Take off your things and put 'em there and sit down." He almost pranced around me. I was not used to such excitement, especially not from a celebrity, and sort of stiffly, numb, I slowly peeled off my heavy coat and fur hat.

Red said, "And look who's here. You know Ann Chidester from Stillwater?"

I said, "Oh yes. We're old friends. Hi, Ann."

"Hi, Fred." She was smiling, and had gotten to her feet, and came over to shake hands. She was a big fine-looking girl with an open honest face and merry watchful eyes.

Red watched us, excited. "My God, isn't he a big lummox, Ann? I thought I was tall, but look at him. My God, he's bigger'n Paul Bunyan himself." Red walked around us like a coach who couldn't believe his eyes. "Well, well. Well, have a seat. Sit down. Now."

We all sat. Red and Ann lit cigarettes, and Ann began to fill in the gap with some remarks. I looked over at him, the social part of me numb but the back part of my brain racing and already beginning to record what I was seeing. I noted, among other things, that he was as lean and as tough-looking as a long string of jerked beef and that he had long talon-ended pale hands and a high doming forehead and quick though cracked lips and swift eyes that seemed to notice everything. He was wearing a tweed suit of what I would call an orange shade that seemed to be a part of his whitening red hair and pale blond skin.

My eyes finally fastened on his face. And the face I saw was a face to haunt one in dreams. It was a face that looked as if it were being slowly ravaged by a fire, by an emotional fire, by a fire that was already fading a little and that was leaving a slowly contracting lump of gray-red cinder.

We talked a few minutes, Ann and I, with Red listening, and watching my eyes and lips, and looking up and down my body, and observing my big wet feet (I still hadn't been able to buy galoshes or rubbers my size) and my big red hands, and then he said suddenly, "What've you got in that package?"

"A couple of books."

"Well? well?" he said, moving on his couch, reaching out a hand, snapping his fingers. "Well, are you going to let me see it?"

I handed the package to him, and his nervous tic-ridden fingers

pulled off the wrapping. He looked. "Good, good," he said, "fine.
Here, you fix up your book for me and I'll fix up my book for you."
I was glad to comply, and I wrote something to the effect that
I regarded him as one of those who had shown the way for the
younger writing generation coming in, had made it possible for
them to relax while they were being honest. He was quite pleased
with the sentiment, and a quick tear came and went in his eyes. He
made a quick move to hide his feelings, and waved his slinging arms
and hands around for us to keep talking. What he wrote for me in
his book made the blood suddenly roar through my head. He wrote
only three words. But they were words a young brave longs to hear
from a chief. And, for my own sanity, they were also words I quickly
shook some salt on.

We sat maybe some five minutes, talking about this, that and the
other, nothing serious that I remember now anyway, when all of a
sudden he got to his feet — I had gotten up to get a handkerchief
from my overcoat — and said, speaking over his shoulder at Ann,
"Isn't he a whopper? Isn't he, isn't he? Look," he said, "look, we've
got to see more of each other. How about you coming up for a
couple of days to my home in Duluth? On a visit? Then we can
talk and talk. Visit. How about it? And you too, Ann. Both of
you." He went into another sort of prancing run around us, waving
his lean, almost luminescent hands, plans tumbling out of his cracked
lips in profusion. "Look, how about next week? Ann, you've got a
good car, so you pick him up. Ah-h, say, come up on Thursday.
And stay as long as you like. A week. Ten days. A whole weekend
at least. That'll be fine. Okay, Fred?"

"Sure, that's fine. If it won't be too much of a bother."

"Bother? bother? Not at all. You must come."

I said, "Uh, Mr. Lewis, would you mind if I took my wife
along?"

"Wife? wife?" A shadow passed over his cinder-tight face. "Wife?"

I laughed. "I'm still at that stage, Mr. Lewis, where I like to share things with my wife. Or maybe I'm just old-fashioned."

"Where do you get that 'mister' stuff, huh? You hate me or somethin', huh? I'm Red to my friends."

"Red, then. Could Maryanna come with me?"

"Oh-h . . . all right. If you must. But Ann will drive you up. Okay, Ann?"

Ann said, "That's fine with me, Red."

"Good, good. That's all set then. Fine."

About then his driver came in for some instructions. Red introduced him as Ace. The driver was a slow-smiling, calm-faced fellow with quiet eyes that sized things up realistically. Red said, "By the way, Ace, the kids here, Ann and Fred, are coming up to spend a week with me. Isn't that wonderful? We'll just have a wonderful time. I need a little life and excitement around me before I start the new book and they'll be just right."

"I see," Ace said, hardly changing expression. "Sounds fine."

"It is fine," Red said, dancing around Ace. "And we'll have a swell time."

After Red had dismissed Ace, he gave us a mischievous look. "Ace's not only the best driver in the state of Minnesota but the most informed. What he don't know about Duluth isn't worth recording. He used to operate a taxi stand there and he ran into all of the stuck-ups at all hours of the night and in all sorts of conditions."

We laughed.

We talked some more, and then finally, noticing that he seemed on edge about something, and thinking perhaps I had used up my first welcome, I made a move to go. Ann got up too. He seemed relieved.

He repeated his invitation in the doorway as we shook hands. "Well, I'll see the two of you next week. Thursday, sometime in the afternoon."

"Fine, Red." To make sure he understood I had his permission to take my wife with me, I said, "It's all right then if Maryanna comes with me?"

"Who?"

"My wife."

"Oh. Her. Well . . . okay. If she must, take her along."

Driving up in the bitter cold, with a good foot of snow lying on the ground, it seemed strange to me that we should be going to visit a quick-tempered, even hot-tempered, man in that cold northland pine country, where the land was always either green or white or both. Even his nickname Red seemed out of place.

We got there in the afternoon, and he held open the door of his banker-class Tudor house and welcomed us in friendly fashion. His housekeeper showed us our rooms. We freshened ourselves and came down, and were invited to have tea with him in the dining room. He took the head of the table, placed Ann on his left, Maryanna on his right, and me across from him — a chair, I remember thinking, that a wife of his should have sat in. The dining room was really a sort of splendid dining hall, with walnut paneling and colored windows and thick carpeting and hand-carved sideboards encircling a red-leather-topped table and red-leather armchairs. The chairs caught my eye in particular because they were the first I had encountered in which I could lounge a little while I ate.

As the tea was being poured by the housekeeper—she had taken a seat to my right for a few moments — Red took a notebook out of his pocket and waited a moment for the talk to die down, then said, "Look, I'd like to get your reaction to these titles." He put down a nervous finger, traced the titles. "Kingson, Kingsblood, Kingsman. Which do you like best for a book that's about a man who believes in a family legend that somewhere way back one of the ancestors descended from royalty? When all along he's really got some Negro blood in him?"

All three of us chose Kingsblood. The unanimity surprised him. He looked around at all of us, nodded, said, "Good. I've got the title for my new book then. And now I can relax for the rest of your stay here. Next week I can begin work."

I had heard before about Red's way of letting others choose his titles for him, and sitting there I had the distinct feeling that he had taken our pulse, that with his finger on the pulse he was again his father, the country bedside doctor, the father he admired to idolatry. And I also had the feeling that Red was asking us to share in the responsibility—some would say guilt—for the kind of books he wrote.

Then he turned over a page in the notebook and looked at me. "Read your *Boy Almighty*. I've been coughing" — he demonstrated — "been coughing ever since. Felt like I really had TB myself. Wonderful. Have only a few adverse comments to offer." He peered down at the notebook. "You've got a little too much bull in it." There was a laugh around the table. He laughed too. "But I mean it. Here." He tore out the sheet and handed it across to me, I looked at it:

> Feikema —
>   Fawkes' notes
>   Excessive virility —
>   manroots
>   bull seeding heifer
>   Wants fellow dreamer
>   P.S. Ace and I got TB.

"Could I keep this?" I asked.

"Of course, course. I want you to keep it. And to take those things and consider 'em. I'm not giving orders, you understand. I just want you to look at it."

Tea finished, Red said he had a few errands to do up in his room. The womenfolk thought they should change for dinner, and I thought that with my TB background I could use a cat nap. Before I went up to our room, Red's housekeeper, buxom, quite self-contained and obviously proud of her position, wanted to show me the place. In the living room she pointed out the "expensive" phonograph radio, the Childe Hassam oils, the massive and "expensive" lamps, the thick rugs, the drapery, the "snappy" chairs; in the solarium she pointed out some choice knickknacks while completely overlooking the walls that were tight with "expensive" sets of books; in the hall she again pointed out come "expensive" lamps while overlooking a couple of cases full of good books; and then, coming to the room where Maryanna and I were to stay, she pointed out some more "expensive" lamps. The lamps seemed to be on her mind, for some reason or other, and to kid her a little, I said, "I ought to snitch one and then I could live easy for a couple of years."

She gave me a hooded look. "Better not play any gags," she said. "They really do cost a lot of money. That one by your bed there cost over two hundred dollars."

I gave her a stare. My wife and I had been managing to get along with a little number over our bed that cost us $1.98 at Sears, Roebuck.

She nodded. "It's true."

"Lady, I'll take care of that lamp as if it were my own child. Don't worry."

The truth is, after that lamp harangue, I was careful not to turn on any lamps except the one in the bathroom. That one, I decided, had been put in by the contractor's electrician and was probably designed for service.

While the women finished dressing, I sat in a chair in front of our second-story window and looked out far across to Lake Superior. Its surface was almost covered with ice, with the center still blue and steaming mightily. I looked down and saw the city of Duluth staggered roof by roof down the high bluff to the water front. It was a mighty sight and I thought to myself, well, maybe Red has found his home at last — because this is a sight that could inspire even a king to poetry.

At the dinner that night he got going on the race question. He had spent some time in the South and had also hired himself a male colored cook named Joseph, a cook who had excellent reading tastes. Red not only seemed to have explored the scenes of racial intolerance, but had also done a lot of reading on the subject. He probed us to see how we reacted to it all, but the only reaction he got from us was agreement. It was obvious, as we went along, that Red's interest was more than just casual, that in fact, as his list of titles suggested, he was about to explore the race question — which he did, of course, in his next novel, *Kingsblood Royal*. Red's way of arguing was to exaggerate a point and then sit back. If anybody was so foolish as to reply exaggeratedly, Red was out and pouncing. And though some new sores along his lips seemed to hurt him when he talked too vigorously, he didn't let his prey get away.

Dishes came and went, and we talked and talked, and finally around nine-thirty we retired to the living room. We sat before a white marble fireplace. Ann and Red hooked up in a furious chess game while the phonograph played Delius. Somehow, it seemed to me at the time, *"Sea Drift"* seemed to fit the mood of the dappled yellow-green Hassams on the wall. The music was soothing to me, though to Red, when he got behind in his chess game, it seemed a stimulant. Ann was a solid player, steady, while Red was inclined to be too daring in the beginning, which put him behind, and then he had to turn on the heat. He was good when pressed. After winning the game, Red indicated he was tired and turned down the house-keeper's offer to serve a nightcap. We all went to bed — the male Feikema careful not to turn on any of the high-priced lamps.

The next few days went along at about the same tempo: meals at regular hours but with a lot of time spent talking afterwards over coffee around the red-topped table while lolling in the huge arm-chairs. We talked of life and letters. Ann was a great storyteller, and she had a way of building up a climax in even the most ordinary of events that made Red listen with his mouth partially open.

Someone happened to mention Mencken, and Red's face clouded. "Yes, Hank was a great guy. Real force. Did a lot of good. And I liked the old Hank. That is, the Hank when he was younger. He was an honest fighter. But lately, he's taken to issuing pronunciamentoes from on high. And that I don't like. Taking him-self entirely too seriously."

Another mentioned Dreiser and what a tower of a man he was. Again Red was disturbed about something and waving his spoon over his cup, he said, "True, true. Dreiser's great, all right. But one thing many people don't know about. He wasn't always for the underdog. Not at all. When he was an editor he was one of the toughest devils to talk to any young writer had to face. Ted was all apple pie to the old successful hack, but when any young punk came in, Dreiser was all teeth. He was like a bulldog defending his mas-ter's, his boss's property. He scared the talent out of many a timid young fellow."

Ann said, "He didn't seem to have scared you."

"Of course not. I fought back. I wasn't afraid of him. The big boob."

Someone mentioned Jim Farrell, saying that he was quite an admirer of Dreiser even though their political religions were in violent opposition at the end. This caused Red to smile in memory and he said, "You know, I have to admire Jim. I gave his latest book a panning in *Esquire*. I said he was writing sloppily, besides thinking sloppily. And what do you know. Sometime later Jim gets a chance to take a crack at me in print and he says, 'Who? Red Lewis? That old hack?' " Red laughed. "He sure whacked me one there."

"Are you going to whack him back?"

"What? Never. We each take a crack and then we quit. Otherwise we're admitting we've been hit bad."

Red added, "Now you kids, when you get bad reviews, let most of 'em go. But somewhere along the line, when you get a chance, and the chance is a good one and you're properly enraged, why then let fly." Red chuckled and daintily touched his sore lips with a voluminous white handkerchief. "Never will forget the way I fixed one fellow. He was an English reviewer. In England. And by great luck we met at a party. He had taken me all apart in his reviews, you know, had just given me a whale of a beating, from one end to the other. I was awful, he said. No art at all. Sheer reporting. Rampant journalism. Wrote enormous fat notebooks. Said I should brood more over my things. Et cetera. Said what I had to say was pure tripe. That the paper it was printed on had been wasted, and so on. I spotted him at this party, then, and so I said to my friend sitting next to me, 'Watch this. I'm going to give this guy the Minnesota treatment.' I introduced myself. When he heard my name, he blinked and took a step back, raising his hands as if he expected me to punch him. Then I turned on the charm. I thanked him profusely for all the wonderful attention he had given me. Told him nobody, not even the American critics, had shown such insight into my work. No one had noticed all the subtle nuances that he had seen. Oh, I just laid it on. Finally my friend jerks my elbow and whispers, 'For godsakes, Red, cut it out. This is killin' me.' "

"What happened?"

Red laughed. "Why, after that I never got better reviews in my life. He became the greatest expert on Red Lewis in Europe."

We talked about Upper Midlands writers, in particular Minnesota writers: Le Sueur, Gray, Seeley, Krause, Beach, Derleth. About Robert Penn Warren, who was teaching at the University of Minnesota, he fell silent. It happened that I had met Red Warren and that I had read his poems and novels. I said that I thought highly of him both as man and as artist. Red Lewis listened with interest. At the time it was difficult to tell if he had read Warren or was keeping his opinion to himself. He did mutter that a writer had to be careful not to get the "literary clique religion," which was just as bad as the Jesus or the Mohammedan or the Lenin religion. That night, when we went to bed, I happened to notice on his bedtable, beside Tolstoi's *Anna Karenina* that he was reading, one of Warren's books. Later, Red Lewis was one of the first to hail Red Warren's new book, *All the King's Men*.

Sitting before the great picture window one evening, watching twilight deepen the steaming grayish-blue of Lake Superior to dark blue, Red fell into a self-belittling mood. It was as if the end of another day had reminded him that eventually it all had to end at last in the endless blue-dark of eternity. "That's the way it goes. For a little while you have it. The old bite, the old sting. And you give it to 'em while you have it. And everybody cheers and everybody says, 'He's really on today, isn't he? He's really hot this time! Wow!' But it isn't long before it's all gone. The vim, the vigor, the celestial spark. All gone." Red continued to look out over the darkening lake in the falling night. "You may kid yourself for a little while that you've still got it, of course. You may even go around with young kids for a time in the hope of picking up a little of their natural fire. You may even give instructions on how the blurbs for your books should be written — and then when they come out, believe the blurbs yourself. But it isn't long before you're shown up." The lake began to resemble an endless waste of honed basalt. "And if it really should happen that your fangs hang on, society will make damn sure to separate you from them. Oh, not by the obvious way of pulling them out by means of the critical pliers, or by means of the censor's scissors. No, no. But by blandishments. By fussy overattention. By studied cajolery." The night came down tight then and at last the lake and the sky were gone, and Red turned in his chair to look at us. "And they do it so subtly and smoothly that the old rattler himself usually doesn't know when he's been defanged. So that every so often, when people get a little too free or gay with the way they handle the old boy, just to show 'em that he's still got it, that he's still dangerous, that he still possesses his old sting, the old boy coils up, and opens his serpent's mouth and hisses, and drums his rattles. And they, remembering how he used to knock 'em dead, they all back away a little again. And murmur and whisper half-fearfully and half-admiringly about how the old boy still can do it. He may even strike a couple of times, hitting live flesh here and there. So that then everybody cheers and shouts, 'By God, he actually really did it again!' " Red let a hand fall from his lap. "But after a while, when none of the stung die, it becomes apparent it was a hollow show. That he didn't have it at all anymore."

We also talked about the great middle class. On this he was quite voluble, saying among other things that the middle class had always been and would always be, and how happy he had been to see that that was what he should write about, since he knew it so well all the way back to his roots — they were his meat, and they

were also his friends. He said, "You know, people just don't understand me. Here I think I've presented a warm picture of the man
Cass Timberlane, and everybody thinks I hate him. Well, if I hate
him I hate myself. Which I don't. At least not that I'm aware of."
And there was one occasion when he did re-enact the role of a
Babbitt. We had not been there more than a day when he told us
that he had decided to leave Duluth, that he had already sold the
house for May delivery, and that he was now engaged in selling
some of the extra furniture which he didn't want to cart across the
country to Massachusetts. Sure enough, when a furniture dealer
showed up to have a look at the things, along with some of the many
rare lamps, Red undertook to do the selling himself. He haggled
and rubbed his hands and jumped up and down and stamped his
feet and gasped in mock amazement at low offers and swept the
dealer with shrewd side looks. And when they had done, he came
back into the solarium, rubbing his hands still, smiling like the cat
that had caught the mouse, exclaiming, "By God, I think I did him
more than he did me." He relished it.

The second night there, he organized a small party. Two of the
guests, a married couple, the Marvin Orecks, were exclusive folk, he
said. "People who because of their race are not welcome in the
homes of the Duluth mighty, the elegant supersnoots. When I first
came to Duluth, I used to hang around a little with Margaret Cul-
kin Banning and the Oliver Mining Company crowd, but when they
wouldn't invite my friends, and especially these two friends, why I
cut 'em. Besides, after the first highball, Margaret always thinks she
has to tell me what's wrong with my novels. When I know better
what's wrong with 'em than she does. Why, one night she tried to
tell Johnny Gunther what he really should have done with his
Insides. Nah, she's too bossy." The other two people to come, Red

said, were a judge and his good wife. "A judge everybody thinks I modeled Cass Timberlane after. Utter nonsense. Not so at all. As you will see when you meet him."

The party was a success at first. We were still lingering over coffee in the luxurious dining room when they arrived, and Red suggested that they all come right in and join us for another cup.

It wasn't long before one of the women mentioned the name of his former wife, Dorothy Thompson, the newspaper columnist. Red's eyes lighted up. Someone said he had heard her give a talk in favor of re-electing Roosevelt, a fighting talk as it turned out, and when the account of it was finished, Red said, hitting the table, "Atta girl, Dotty. Give it to 'em!"

We all smiled. He really still liked her. Red said, "Yes, Dorothy was a great gal. A wonderful gal. If only she hadn't been so damn bossy." He sighed deeply. "But . . . she being what she was, she just had to be bossy. Too bossy. That poor fellow she's married to now, I sure pity him. I hear he's a sculptor. Huh. I can just imagine the kind of life that poor devil leads. Just imagine it. Henry . . ." Red paused, gave us a look. "Henry is as good a name as any. Henry wakes up in the morning to the sound of Dorothy's 'Henry! Henry! time to get up and have your grapefruit now. Get into your clothes and wash your hands and come down.' A little later, when she's about to drive off to the great city of New York she calls into the breakfast nook, 'Henry! Henry! time for you to go off to your work now, you know. Come come.' And she leads him to the barn where he's got his marble and chisels and hammer and she opens the door and says, 'All right, Henry, get in there and sculpt now. And when I come back I want you to have another piece finished, you know,' and then she locks him in. When she comes home at night, she unlocks the door and looks in and asks, 'Well, Henry, did you finish your piece today?' And by heavens, he'd better be able to show a few new chisel marks somewhere on some stone or you know what he gets. Uh-huh. She'll say, 'You get back in there and sculpt, you miserable little worm! You haven't even earned your breakfast yet. Let alone your lunch and dinner.' And she locks him in again."

There was much laughter around the table.

He peered around at all of us, to see what the effect had been. Seeing that Ann was laughing the loudest, Red suddenly turned on her. "And you. Look at you. Built just like her. Husky. Vigorous. Strapping and powerful. Clear-eyed Brunhilde all over again. Got a lot of strong opinions. And you write too. And you do what you want. Oh-h, I sure pity the guy you marry. You'll treat that poor bugger just like Dorothy treats that poor man." He lashed out a long yellow finger at Ann. "Why don't you leave us poor little fellows alone? We're only trying to get along the best we can. In our little way." He looked over at me to include me in the talk. "We're only trying to get along like honest men. Fred and me. We're harmless. We don't mean any harm. But here you big American women come along and beat us up and lock us up and baby-feed us from dawn to sunset. When you give us your opinion you raise your voice and beat the table like any fool of a man. My good-ness, woman, let us have some freedom. So we get a chance to grow up. First thing you know, the little will power we have left will be completely atrophied in us. Please."

We laughed harder than ever, Ann still hardest. She was choking with it. Red was in fine form and knew it.

"Yeah, you American women. I know a certain Midland college president. Famous fellow. Great administrator — probably gets more brilliant ideas per day than his entire faculty combined. But the poor bugger's doomed. He's married to an American woman. And you know what she does? Besides wishing she were back in the good old days when she was a foetus? He isn't awake one minute but what she hasn't pricked his balloon. You know how a man is in the morning. After he's washed the sleep out of his eyes, and is sipping at his coffee, why, he slowly starts getting a few ideas on how he's to face the day. Ideas at that time are very delicate and uncertain. They need to be encouraged. They need warmth and love. Gentle love. So here he is, the poor sucker, warming his hands around his cup of coffee, savoring it, feeling the warmth of it rising in his nostrils, and slowly but surely becoming aware of a few timid little morning notions in his head, and vaguely hoping that these little timid creatures may grow up . . . when all of a sudden his hag of a wife has to mention some horrible personal defect of his, some trivial little thing that sticks him in the soft spot, that only she could know because she dresses and undresses on the opposite side of the bed from him. And wheeet! Gone are the little timid embryo ideas for that day. How that man has refrained from poisoning her is beyond me. Beyond me. No, most modern American women are ruined. Ruined."

There was some more laughter, mostly from the males.

"Yeah, and I'm the only male here who can talk up. The rest of you bums are married and 're scared of what your wife will do to you when you go to bed tonight."

More laughter, this time uneasily from the men.

The judge's wife couldn't let the hot ember lie, and she challenged him. "Oh now, Mr. Lewis, you know that's exaggerated."

He leaped up, a yellow fire, finger darting like a licking flame. "What d'you mean, 'exaggerated'? Of course it's not exaggerated. American women are like that. Killers of talent. Unless it's talent which helps them obtain power. But the minute it's talent that they can't control or understand, why, stab stab stab, they've got to prick that balloon. The . . . the . . . of course they're like that."

"Oh come now."

Red jumped about a foot. And suddenly he kicked back his chair and whirled and lunged out of the room and tramped upstairs to his den.

An appalling silence fell over us. Our host had left us.

Finally Ann said, trying to pull the gap together again. "It's all my fault. I shouldn't've laughed so hard when he was teasing me."

"No no," the judge's wife said. "No no, it's my fault." She turned very red. She put a hand to her face and hid her eyes. "What do we do now?"

For the moment no one had an idea. We all toyed with our spoons, clinking the coffee cups a little.

The judge's wife said, "God, I feel awful."

It just happened that Red's calm-faced driver, Ace, had joined us some ten minutes before (Red had the custom of getting his cook, driver, and housekeeper into all sorts of discussions with his guests — it was probably one of his ways of getting interesting reactions), and he said simply, "Just let him alone. Give him time to cool off. He'll be back. Keep talking down here as if nothing happened. I've been around him long enough and I know that'll do it. He's quick-tempered but he's also a quick forgiver."

If Red was a quick forgiver, I thought to myself, why did he still think the way he did about American women? It was either a case of an irascible temper or a case of extreme provocation. Or both.

"God, I feel awful," the judge's wife said. She made moves to get up and go home. Her husband the judge held her down.

Ann asked me, "What do we do now? These people can go home but we're staying at his house."

"I dunno. Follow Ace's advice I guess." I tried to smile. "Furthermore, for myself, I don't think I've done anything to feel guilty about. My God, we're allowed private opinions on these things, aren't we? That you feel you shouldn't laugh so loud is all wrong. You're letting him move in on you."

"God, I feel awful," the judge's wife said.

Sure enough, after we had managed to knit some sort of conversation together again, all the while very aware of his pacing directly above us, we heard him coming down the stairs and then shuffling through the hall. He came in diffidently, almost like a little boy, a little boy who was having a hard time admitting he had been in the wrong. He stood at the head of the table and looked at all of us, each of us, and then apologized very graciously, almost sweetly, and as he drew up his chair and sat down, he turned to the red-faced judge's wife. "Really, my dear, you know I'm touchy on that subject. Why did you have to stir me up? You know that you shouldn't've stirred that old knife that's still sticking in me."

Slowly the talk picked up again, and the embarrassed judge's wife got back her original coloring, and Red let loose more and more, and by the time the party broke up, it was as if the blowup had never been. Everyone was gaily bidding everyone else good night.

The next day Ann happened to find, in one of the guest rooms, a bookcase full of first editions, foreign editions, special editions of all Red's work. Red's reaction was one of shyness. He refused to talk about the books, and after a moment or two, led us away.

Apparently, however, the incident served to warm him up to something, and it wasn't long before he had me in his workroom showing me how he did his writing. (Ann apparently had been given the same kindness at an earlier date.) He showed me how he laid out his plots, even to building a miniature city with the main house or setting especially set up in detail. He let me page through his notebooks, telling me about his manner of collecting and note-taking. He let me see his notebook containing the master list of the names of all characters he had ever used. He showed me a sample of his first draft, second draft with corrections, and his third draft. Then, he said, he always tried to get someone to read the whole book back to him. And, at the very last, he copied the final draft himself. "Because I always find something which no stenographer on earth would find."

As he talked he was very careful to stress that these were his methods, worked out painfully over a long period of time, and that I was not to think that I should follow them even remotely. "Work out your own system that fits you, and t'hell with everybody else's system. You're the only one that knows what's right for you. That is, if you've got the brains."

This led later on into his questioning about my publisher, the Itasca Press. We were having dinner at the time.

"How come you got published by a Midland outfit in St. Paul there?"

"Well . . . because the editor there, Paul Hillestad, was willing to work with me, while the Eastern dodos would either say nothing or tell me vaguely to rewrite."

"Maybe they were right."

"Never. They complained about my dialogue. Said no one talked that way. Well, it just happens, Red, that that's the one thing I've really got. An ear for speech and sound. I defy anybody to beat it."

Red's eyes opened at this and he smiled a little.

"They tried to tell me I should see how Steinbeck did his Okies. That really made me roar, because it was my considered opinion that Steinbeck did not quite get those Okies. What he had was partially affected. And I don't mean artistically, because that might be all right. He listened to the Okies in California, all right, but he got so lousy sentimental he read sounds into their mouths they could never have uttered." I snorted. "Then these same dodos suggested I go see how Hemingway did it. I said I wasn't sure Hemingway had caught it either. To me he has the sound of a man who has spent too much time listening to a bunch of barroom bums just sober enough to mutter monosyllables. Or maybe too much time listening to himself say truly yes and truly no."

Red laughed.

"At any rate, Paul Hillestad let my real stuff alone. And Paul took the time to read over every line with me and made me fight to keep it. I learned to write with that fellow. And I now defy anyone to take one line out of any one of my books. That anyone had better have an armful of reasons if he tries it, because I've always got that many for keeping it in — besides feeling that it should stay in."

Red nodded. "Well, that's all very well and all. But now it's time for you to go to an Eastern house and get distribution."

"Maybe the Itasca Press can get that for me too."

"Nah. Got to have a big house in the East. They're the only ones who can do that for you. You've got to have distribution, audience reaction. Got to know that what you are saying is hitting. Otherwise you're writing in a wilderness, in a vacuum. To nobody. Got to have that finger right on that pulse or else you're missing it."

"But, Red, I don't like leaving Paul just like that. We're friends. I couldn't just pull out and leave just because I want to go out and make a lot of money."

"Well, if you're friends and 're afraid you'll get softhearted, write him a letter and point-blank tell him to send it back to you by mail."

"Oh, but you can't do that to a friend, man!"

Red leaped up, shoving back his chair. " 'Friend'? You a friend with a publisher? Are you mad? Never be close friends with a publisher. They get the notion they're married to you then. Can boss you around. Nah. Publishers are peddlers. Book peddlers. You write 'em, and they peddle 'em. Publishers are supposed to be commercial. They don't write books. Couldn't. Or else they would."

"I dunno, Red. Paul is an awful good friend of mine."

He stared at me, eyes reddening a little. Then he shot a look at Maryanna sitting to his right, and asked, "Fred and this Hillestad guy, they aren't married, are they?"

Maryanna laughed. "No. But they do like each other."

"Terrible mistake. Always keep your publisher at a distance. Especially the editor." Red sat down again, went into a lengthy history of his own relations with Harcourt, Brace, with Doubleday, and finally Random House. He had kind words only for the latter. I couldn't help remembering that the last named was his current publisher.

Red sat down again. "Look, I'm not going to have you remain buried out here with a Midland outfit. I'll fix you up a letter to my agent Alan C. Collins and he'll get you into a new house — a big one in the East."

"I'll first have to talk to Paul. A man just doesn't walk out without some explanation. Besides, I'm not sure I want to leave. That's to be my decision."

Red jumped up again. This time I thought I was going to get the red-faced woman's treatment. "No no no, you have to go East! You've got to get your stuff out. New York is the publishing center. Not the Twin Cities. All the Twin Cities is known for is flour milling. It's not the book center. You're going at this all wrong. You big bullheaded Dutchman."

"I'm a stiff-necked Frisian."

"What's the difference? Frisian, Dutchman, it's all the same."

"Oh no. Calling a Frisian a Dutchman is like calling an Irishman an Englishman."

"Anyway, you've got to go East." With that, Red strode out of the room.

Some ten minutes later he came back with a letter. He handed it to me.

"Read it."

It was to his agent, saying that he was instructing me to send him my next book, *This Is the Year*, almost finished. The letter was emphatic, almost written like a military command.

Red was slowly but surely taking and making me over. He began to act like a possessive father to me, as if I were a sort of balky, stubborn son who needed a little harnessing and stropping to get into line. He even bothered to check up on my manners—telling me, for example, that I shouldn't talk with my hand over my mouth (a habit I had whenever I wasn't sure of myself), that I should wear conservative clothes since I stuck out enough as it was, that I should watch my health like a hawk, what with having a tubercular history. And in a way, I liked the attention. Heretofore I'd had to battle everything out alone. My own relatives weren't too eager about my wanting to write, and there wasn't one of them who was capable of any sort of advice, even bad. The final result was that I did go East. But only after I had told everything to Paul and only after he had assured me that he wanted me to follow whatever course would prove best for me.

We were talking in the library the last day. We were to leave shortly.

Suddenly Red said, looking over at my wife as she stood beside a bookcase, "Maryanna, come here. Come here."

She went near him, almost warily.

He took her hand and kissed it. "Maryanna, at first I didn't know about this business of Fred being married. But having seen you for a couple of days now I know you're just right for him. Just right." He kissed her hand again. "Fine woman, fine woman. And Fred, you be good to her. And listen to her advice. She knows what's best."

This made me smile. I had been careful not to tell Maryanna about Red's frown when I'd asked if she could go along. Also, Maryanna happens to be one of the most sympathetic listeners in captivity, and, true to her nature, throughout the visit she had confined herself to a few brief, telling remarks salted in at the right places.

"Remember now," he said.

Then it was time to go. I was first to get ready, and came downstairs where he was waiting. I carried our suitcases. The others were still chatting upstairs, finishing their dressing for the cold and the road. It was below zero outside.

I stood near the door with fur cap in hand, big coat on. Red paced back and forth in front of a long table, where a mail tray and a big lamp had been placed on a runner. He walked with head down, hands folded behind him. His long silk robe rustled.

Abruptly he broke off his pacing. He came up to me and gave me a long under-the-brow look, and then punched me lightly and playfully in the belly. "Look at you. A great big fellow. With your whole life still before you. With the whole wide world still to conquer — when, from that height, it's already at your feet. A lot of world because you stand tall."

I protested a little. "Some have thought my tallness a hindrance."

"Who?"

"Well, I'm not too sure my wife's accepted it. Out on the dance floor, for example. Sitting down, yes."

"Have you accepted it?"

"Yes."

"Does it bother you?"

"Not any more."

"Look. Don't trip over your own strength. Like I did for a while over mine."

"You?"

He pointed to his ravaged face. "Yes, me." A look came over his features then, as if he hated what he was going to say, because it was self-pity and he despised self-pity. "There was a time in my life when I was sure that with this to look at, anybody who said they loved me were liars — said it because they had to."

I swallowed. I didn't know what to say. What was there to say to a remark like that?

He punched me lightly in the belly again, and he mellowed, and he said, "Work. Work. Work. And it'll all bend before you."

Then the women came down and it was time to go. He threw his arms around both Maryanna and Ann, gripped my hand.

I saw him three times after that: once at a party given by a University of Minnesota professor; later in his rooms in the St. Paul Hotel, where he entertained Ann and Maryanna and me along with another young man who wanted to write; and then later in his rooms at the Algonquin in New York City. Except for one short spell, he didn't have much to say, and that exception had to do with a parody of the old-time Bible-pounding hell-and-damnation preacher — something he was looking into since he was already working on *The God-Seeker*.

Once some University of Minnesota students, who were planning to put out a literary quarterly, asked me if I wouldn't write to ask him for a contribution of some sort. In the same letter, knowing he would be interested, I told him of my own plans.

His answer was characteristic:

> Thorvale Farm
> Williamstown, Mass.
> November 3, 1945

Dear Fred:

The Chokecherry Tree and *World's Wanderer** sound grand, and I rejoice in them. The North Star Review sounds terrible — just like every other of the 10,000 Lil Magazines of the past 30 years. It will probably be lots of fun, and a complete waste of time and money, but parental advice never did keep the lusty young man from dumb girl. I might, however, faintly whisper that a novelist's job is to write novels, not try to compete with professional magazine publishers.

Ever,

Red

January 26, 1951
At Wrâlda

I was in bed with the flu late in January, 1951, when the phone rang. It was Chuck Rathe, editor of the *Sauk Centre Herald*, asking if I had heard that Sinclair Lewis had died in Rome. I said, yes, I had. Well then, he said, would you consider giving an address or some kind of eulogy at his funeral to be held in Sauk Centre, January 28, 1951?

My first thought was to say no. I don't particularly like funerals. I knew Red Lewis had requested that there be no religious service at his funeral. I also recalled an earlier time when Red and I had discussed whether or not he should go to his brother Fred's funeral and that he had not gone.

Rathe went on to explain that Red's brother, Dr. Claude Lewis, had asked him to find someone to give an address or a talk at the funeral and that he in turn had called Thomas Barnhart, professor of journalism, at the University of Minnesota. Barnhart said there was only one candidate and that was another Minnesota novelist. "And that's you, Fred."

Rathe urged me to accept. It was a special request by the Lewis

* Later on titled *Wanderlust*.

family. Also someone had better speak up for Red in his home state. I finally decided to go.

So while recovering from the flu the next week, mostly in bed, I began composing what I might say. Trouble was that though I admired Sinclair Lewis very much, and valued his great contribution to American literature, he was not my kind of writer. He'd had no direct influence on my writing. His book *Elmer Gantry* had meant a lot to me while in college, mostly to help me make up my mind about certain aspects of religion. I knew also that he had once recommended that I be given a grant-in-aid from the American Academy of Arts and Letters. Further, I'd been his guest for a week in Duluth and we'd got along very well. But he belonged to the cat family of writers and I to the bear family. (He liked cats for pets and I liked dogs.) So anything I would have to say would have to be qualified. Red would want me to speak my mind about him. Thus when it came to the question as to what I thought of him as a writer, I finally said in the eulogy, "We have here an example of how emotional force and mental brilliance lifted and developed an ordinary talent into greatness — something we also find in the case of his famous contemporary, Theodore Dreiser." * It was going to be a hard thing to say in front of his family and friends. But I said it. Today I still feel that Red Lewis wasn't first of all a novelist, that his real talent lay elsewhere, if not in satire and caricature, then in science. He wasn't a natural bard or storyteller. But he was so brilliant that with one of the lesser of his talents he could still speak out with a powerful voice.

A young newspaperman, Bob Markson of Minneapolis, drove my wife and me up to Sauk Centre on Sunday, January 28. It was twenty-six below zero that morning in Minneapolis. When we arrived at the high school that noon, everybody was complaining

* See page 139 below for the full text of the eulogy.

about the terrible cold weather. There was a good crowd out, though, mostly from the area, which I thought remarkable after all the mean things Red was supposed to have said about Sauk Centre. Lewis's editor Harry E. Maule of Random House was there. Son Michael Lewis had flown in. And of course newspapermen and newscasters had also come.

I read the eulogy in a squeaky voice. The cold weather wasn't helping my throat any. Below the lectern, in a silver urn on a small table, were Lewis's ashes. I couldn't help but glance at them now and then as I read along. Strange thoughts shot through my mind about them and several times I thought of throwing the written eulogy away and of speaking those thoughts.

An hour later we were out at the cemetery. A stack of some of Lewis's books had been placed in a small square hole dug into the Lewis family plot. It was still bitterly cold, twenty-two below zero. Luckily there was little or no wind out, or the chill factor, as weathermen say nowdays, would have been intolerable, especially for one recovering from the flu. Yet I have no recollection of any real discomfort.

I stood behind members of the family as Dr. Claude Lewis with a scissors snipped the red ribbon seals on the silver urn, opened the urn, and poured the ashes over the books in the grave. There was a difference of some 90 degrees between the warmth caught inside the urn (it had just come out of the warm high school) and the fierce cold outdoors, and the moment the urn was opened a plume of steam resembling a big puff of human breath rose out of it, as if someone had had to cough because of the cold. The plume of steam rose swiftly, and then, as the light wind from the west caught it, it began to wisp off to the east, very slowly.

Watching the plume go, I couldn't help but remark, mostly to myself, "Well, they tried to bring Red home, but at the last second there he still got away." I was overheard. Chuck Rathe turned and gave me an appreciative look.

I mention what happened at the grave site in some detail because of what occurred some years later. William Van O'Connor called me one day and asked me if I cared to go along with him and Malcolm Cowley to Sauk Centre where Cowley was to give an address at a dinner given in honor of Sinclair Lewis. I said I'd like to go very much. We drove up in Van O'Connor's car, with Bill driving and Cowley seated next to him and I in the back seat leaning forward to make cozy talk all the way up.

As we approached Sauk Centre, Cowley expressed the wish to see Red's grave before we met the people in Sauk Centre. I showed them the way. While there, I described the above burial scene, waving my hands a little to make it the more vivid. Cowley was moved. "Poor Red," he said.

That night midway in his talk, Cowley paused, looked down at where I sat, and then said, to illustrate his point that Lewis had trouble settling down anywhere, "Yes, and when he was buried here in Sauk Centre he apparently still had trouble settling down. As my friend Frederick Manfred so eloquently described it to me out there in the cemetery this afternoon, just as his ashes were being poured into his little grave, a gust of wind came up and blew the ashes all over the prairie."

I was dumbfounded. That wasn't at all what I'd said. I looked over at where Van O'Connor was sitting and he shrugged his shoulders as if to say he couldn't believe what he was hearing either.

Later on I found out that Cowley was hard of hearing. But that's how the story got started that a gust of wind blew Sinclair Lewis's ashes all over Stearns County. The Cowley version is an interesting one. And had it really happened it would be a good story. But the real story is a better one.

May 24, 1969
At Blue Mound

The Artist as the True Child of God

IN THE FEBRUARY 4, 1973, ISSUE OF *The New York Times Book Review*, a man named Wilfrid Sheed wrote an essay entitled "Writer as Wretch and Rat" that caught my eye. It reminded me of what our domeny in Doon, Iowa, had once told me when I'd let slip that I wanted to become a writer.

"That way lies the road to hell," Domeny said gravely. "Writers, painters, all such ilk are a bad lot. Why don't you instead aspire to become a minister? Or a missionary to the heathen? A minister, or a missionary, now they are the true children of God."

Mr. Sheed's remarks told me once again that artists generally have a bad press. And it was startling to see the remarks published in a literary journal, where, of all places, an artist could be expected to get a fair shake.

I guess I've known all the wrong writers. Or else happened to catch them all when they were on their best behavior.

Take Robert Penn Warren. The phone rang one day in early 1943 as I was still trying to get my first novel published. It was Red Warren asking if he could talk to me sometime. The voice was Southern and I had trouble at first catching all the syllables. He said he'd read a recent article of mine in *The New Republic* on Minnesota politics (the rise of both Harold Stassen and Hubert Horatio Humphrey) and he felt that I could help him with some background material he needed for a novel he was writing (*All the King's Men*). We set a date, and then began a series of talks as well as long walks in beautiful Minneapolis, along the banks of the Mississippi River and along the beaches of Lake Harriet, during which Red pumped me for what I could remember about Governor Floyd B. Olson, Governor Elmer Benson, Stassen, Humphrey, Mayor Klein, other local conservatives, liberals, leftists. I'd been a reporter for the old *Minneapolis Journal* as well as a Farmer-Laborite, and had at one time or other run into most of them. Usually Red Warren and I would wind up in his house, where over hot buttered rum we went into depth about motivations, backgrounds, ethnic factors, the like. I didn't mind telling him everything I could remember because I knew that when I got around to writing about politics I'd take an entirely different tack. I was interested in helping him make a good novel as well as a true novel.

As we went along, Red would every now and then suggest that I look into the work of certain other writers, Kenneth Burke, John Crowe Ransom, Alan Swallow, Allen Tate, Donald Davidson, Katherine Anne Porter, William Faulkner, to broaden my knowledge of American letters. When on a couple of occasions I expressed doubt that I'd ever get my first novel published, he spoke of it as if it were a foregone conclusion that it would be. No question about it.

I was in awe of Red when we first met. I was gauche at times. But Red's manners were such it was as if he didn't notice. He let me know he thought I was pretty good in my own right. What really convinced me was the night at a party in Minneapolis (just off Mt. Curve Avenue) when he and I were listening to a university scientist expatiate on the state of all knowledge. With a wink Red said to me, "I suppose we should fall silent while our honored professor roves over the fields of knowledge." It was said with a forgiving smile. It helped me place things in their proper perspective.

It also reassured me as to my own rank. I owe Red one for that.

Over the years I saw Red at many parties, luncheons, stag affairs. Never in all that time did I hear him make a mean or a malicious remark about another writer. There was no doubt that at times he had negative thoughts about some of them, but he kept those thoughts to himself. He appeared to have the same philosophy I had — if you finally must speak up, can't shut up, be generous about what you say of others. Red's behavior to all men, and to all women, was that of a warm and courteous man. As my father used to say of a man he admired, "He was a prince of a fellow."

And at no time did we ever discuss how to make money.

Take John Dos Passos. A friend of mine in Minneapolis, Abbott Washburn, called me one day to ask if I'd like to go along with him and Dos Passos on a little jaunt up to Duluth and into the north country. Dos Passos was investigating the operation of General Mills and Abbott was showing him the various plants the company owned. Abbott, as public relations director for General Mills, had invited him to come to Minnesota.

I spent a week with Dos Passos and Washburn. We made the Spaulding Hotel our headquarters. We visited iron ore mines, the Arrowhead Country, the north shore drive along Lake Superior, the giant elevators in Duluth, the harbormaster.

When Dos Passos learned I'd once stayed for three weeks alone in a cabin deep in the forest, he had to see it. And once he saw it, with great animation, he urged Abbott to help me buy it. He said he could see why I'd been able to write some hundred good pages in three weeks' time in that idyllic spot.

John Dos Passos had a good mind and it ranged in many directions. He was open with his knowledge, sharing it without reservation. No holds barred in friendly exchange. I felt I could say anything in his presence, go in any direction without fear of censure, as rapidly or as slowly as I wanted to. He was warm, courteous, interested. Talk with him, as well as with Warren and Lewis, reminded me of that golden time when I'd first read Plato's *Dialogues*. Being with those men was the good life. They were big.

Never once did I hear Dos Passos make an invidious remark about other writers. When someone brought up Fitzgerald's drinking problem, Dos Passos was quick to explore the strong points of Fitzgerald's writing.

At no time did I hear him discuss money and how to make it. (Abbott told me later on that when he was dealing with Dos Passos on how much Dos Passos would charge General Mills for the article he was writing for them, he had one price and that was it. No haggling.)

Take Meridel Le Sueur. I was told, when I got the first draft of my first novel finished, that I should let Meridel read it. She could help me. I finally did look her up and she did read the manuscript. We met to talk about it in the old Stockholm Cafe on Washington Avenue in Minneapolis. We each had a ham sandwich and a beer. I waited for her to begin. But first she was interested in other things: where did I come from, why did I want to write, what did I like to read, what did I think of my father and mother. After a while I began to get excited. The questions meant that there probably was some merit in the manuscript.

Finally, just as we were about to leave, she picked up the manuscript (which later became my first novel, *The Golden Bowl*) and said, "I've read it. I can't help you. You're one of those writers who has to work it out alone. Never take advice from any other writer. It can only hurt you. Only you will be able to recognize your own mistakes — if you make any. You're your own man. You're too different, too singular, for anyone to help you. Just keep writing and it'll eventually bend for you. Already you've written a book that ranks with the best of Steinbeck."

Meridel was a warm bard-woman. She stressed a writer's good points. I got the feeling from her that she believed negative criticism killed young writers; and that if she privately had misgivings about one's work she didn't mention them on the grounds that silence was the best criticism.

Again, money was never mentioned.

Take Vardis Fisher, that lonely giant of Idaho. Alan Swallow, poet, publisher in Denver, arranged for us to get acquainted, and one day Vardis and his wife Opal dropped in for a visit at Wrâlda, our home at that time in Bloomington, Minnesota. I'd heard that he too was a difficult man to get along with. One look and I could see that he was tough and strong all right, that he had a mind that could pierce into you like an icicle.

But he was considerate. When he saw that I was still weak from a rough bout with the flu, he suggested we all go to bed early so that I could get my rest. The next morning, with my chest feeling much better, we opened our hands to each other. When he said sharp things about other writers, as he did about Thomas Wolfe, he was quick to balance it with gentle things. He too had a far-ranging mind. He and I didn't agree about women, but we indulged each other with our opinions. He said it was the woman in man that made him a novelist. I said it was the man in the woman that made her a novelist. (It is what I believed at the time. The trouble is women until recently have been too busy giving birth and rearing families to write novels. It will be interesting to see, given their new freedom, if women will now write novels as "women" and not write them in imitation of men novelists.) No mean remarks were exchanged.

Later on my wife and I visited Vardis and Opal in their Idaho home, a home he built mostly with his own hands in a hostile arid land. Again there was lively and swift and high conversation, about the Greeks, about Indians, about pioneers, about star systems, about the great composers. Here was another one with whom I could let go, whimsy or lusty comment, with no fear of being looked at as "wretch and rat." Free exchange utterly given. Only once did I detect he was about to say something adverse about Walter Van Tilburg Clark; but in mid-sentence he abruptly began to speak of Walter's strong points.

He made only one comment about money. "Fred, artists are children when it comes to dealing with the commercial world."

Take Walter Van Tilburg Clark. I saw him twice, both times in his home outside Reno, Nevada. In deference to my not caring much for liquor, he instead asked his wife to start us off with black coffee. He spoke his mind, freely; expected me to speak mine, freely. He went out of his way to make me, his guest, feel at home. He made it a point to make sure I got a fair shake in conversation time.

On one of my visits I stayed overnight and he let me sleep in his study. Completely at ease, smiling, we exchanged paperback versions of our work, with the unspoken understanding that there'd be no comment about them. There were too many other things to discuss, both profane and sacred; about the spirit of this old American place, and how we could become the voice for it.

Nothing was said about money. Both of us, smiling a little, lamented that we wouldn't be able to live long enough to get all the work in.

Or Frank Waters. When I was invited to stay with him for several days in his little hacienda at the foot of Blue Mountain near Taos, New Mexico, it was as if his house was more mine than his. He insisted that I sleep in his bed while he slept on a cot in the kitchen. When he discovered that I had an open mind about Indian telepathy and the Indian's primordial sense of life, he broke off work and spent several days exploring Indian ideas and Indian life with me. He was willing, even eager, to open all the drawers of his mind, and anxious for me to do the same, so that we might come to some new discoveries together.

Later he came to visit me in Siouxland. He first wanted to see the Pipestone National Monument where Indians of old, from all quarters of our continent, quarried pipestone for their peace pipes. He was mildly impressed. But when he came to visit me up on the Blue Mounds, an escarpment of an old mountain butt overlooking the prairies to all sides, he fell silent, and his face took on the cast of an Arab looking upon Mecca. My wife wondered if she'd offended him, he was so silent. Me, I liked it. It told me that his feelers had picked up exactly what that eruption of Sioux Quartzite rock was — a place of worship for ancient Indians. When he left he said, "Fred, you have built your house on a sacred place. Let the spirit of the place talk to you. Consider yourself blessed."

On another occasion he wrote a letter to share with me his delight in having spent several days with Vardis Fisher and what a great man he thought Vardis was. The letter told me again that writers are brothers and sisters, that they are beings who try to illuminate human experience and who try to heighten human enjoyment despite The Darks.

Again, no talk about money. No bitterness.

Or take Henry Miller and Max Eastman. Once, while visiting with Frank Gruber and his wife in their little bookstore in Pacific Palisades, California, in 1963, I happened to see a small skinny man on a bicycle flit past their store window. The skinny fellow was riding a ten-speed bike, handlebars forward and down, cap on tight over dark glasses, and going like he was on the last lap of a race and out to win. I laughed a little at the vision of that gnome-like man speeding by and wondered idly who it might be.

"That's Henry Miller," Frank Gruber said.

"The *Tropics* man?"

"The same."

"I thought he lived up in the Big Sur country."

"He's moved down here. Lives a couple of blocks away."

"For goodness sake." Then, musing to myself, I said, "I once corresponded with him. When he first came back to America from Paris. I even have some water colors he sent me. Plus some books of his he sent me."

Gruber was impressed. "You should look him up."

For sheer smooth American style, Henry Miller is one of the best writers we've ever developed. He is unlike all other American writers. I'd looked into him and enjoyed reading him immensely. But I also felt there was a lack in his work. It was too confessional for me, most of it. Henry didn't seem to know how to make or plot a novel. Or else didn't care about plots. I finally said, "He's probably bothered to death by pushy fans."

"He stops in here once in a while. Great guy."

"Think he'd care if I called on him?"

"If you've corresponded with him, he'd probably be glad to meet you," Gruber said.

I hesitated. I was the one who'd dropped the correspondence.

"Shall I tell him that you asked about him?"

"No. I'll get in touch with him. You know his address?"

Gruber's wife dug out Miller's address and telephone number.

A few days later I wrote Henry Miller a note. I reminded him of our previous correspondence. I said I was staying nearby at the Huntington Hartford Foundation. I told him I wouldn't be staying at the Foundation forever, so if we were to meet it had better be soon.

The next day, when I went to get my mail at noon, I found a

telegram in my box. Concerned, thinking it might be bad news from home, I tore it open. It was from Henry Miller, saying that by all means he'd like to see me the coming Friday afternoon.

I let slip to Storm Townsend, a fellow at the Foundation and a sculptress, who was making a bust of me, that I was going to be seeing Miller in a couple of days. Max Eastman, who was also a fellow at the Foundation at the time, writing his autobiography, perked up when Storm joshed me about it at the dinner table as she and I were lingering over our tea.

Max bent kindly blue eyes on me. "You really are going to see Henry Miller?"

"Yes. Friday afternoon."

He fell to musing. "Now there's one man I've always wanted to meet. I've met a lot of the others but never Henry."

"Why don't you come along with me?"

"Oh, but that would be intruding."

"Not at all. I'd enjoy that." Privately I was thinking that having Max along would make it easier meeting Henry. I thought it might be great fun to see those two hoary old boars talking together.

I'd come to like Max Eastman. He was the dean of the dining room table and everybody deferred to him. His young wife was staying with him at the Foundation, which was unusual, since the Foundation rarely let man and wife take up residency at the same time. But she was helping him type up his autobiography and it was specially ruled she too was working on a literary project. When I first met Max I didn't have much to say to him. I'd liked his *Enjoyment of Laughter*. He was of an older generation and I was careful to be respectful around him.

Sometimes he made strong pronouncements at the dinner table. Only a few dared question him. When he turned loose his considerable encyclopedic mind he usually overwhelmed one.

After a while Max noticed that I rarely had any rejoinders to his pronouncements; only sat smiling. Finally one evening he said, "I wonder what our friend Frederick is thinking there at his end of the table."

With a laugh, I said, "Nothing of any moment."

He inclined his gray leonine head with his pink cheeks at me, blue eyes twinkling. "What an interesting use of that word 'moment'. But what were you really thinking?"

He'd been talking about the attitude of the Russians toward us, that they were hostile, and that America had better be on guard. I finally said, "Well, if the USA and the USSR can keep from fighting each other in the next fifty years, succeeding generations will take care of the tensions between them."

"How so?"

"You may repress a people for a few generations, but there'll finally come a time when some one generation will rupture loose. Especially if you teach them how to read. The Russians have been trying hard to cut down on illiteracy, and a generation will finally come, no matter what the oppression is, who will demand to read everything."

He thought about that a while. And after that he always looked over at where I sat to see what I might be thinking. Or smiling about.

Max said, "Well, if we go Friday afternoon, I can just make it. My wife and I are planning to leave Saturday noon by plane."

The next day I got a telephoned note from Henry Miller saying he'd like to postpone my visit to Saturday morning at nine. He'd explain why when I got there.

I walked up to Max Eastman's studio on the ridge.

Max greeted the news with a frown. "But my wife and I are leaving Saturday."

"Can't you still sneak it in? When does your plane leave?"

After some consultation with his young wife, Max finally saw where he could still see Henry. But we'd have to be back by noon. Sharp.

I drove Max over in my old yellow monster Buick. We found Miller's home on Ocampo. I got out, Max following me. I rapped on the door.

Presently the little gnome of a man I'd seen flitting past Gruber's book store appeared in the doorway. He looked up at my height with a widening smile.

"I'm Frederick Manfred. And I have a surprise for you. Max Eastman has been staying at the Foundation with me and he said he'd always wanted to meet you. So I took him along."

Henry's face opened with an even wider smile. He had thick sexy lips. "Max Eastman? Really? Why, and I've always wanted to meet him. All my life. Come in, come in."

We stepped into a short hallway decorated with some of Henry's wild art work. There wasn't a stick of furniture to be seen.

With a laugh, Henry said, "Yeh, that's the reason I had to postpone our meeting until this morning. All of sudden yesterday my young wife decided to leave me. And she hauled out all the furniture, and took the kids, and disappeared. It would have been a little awkward having you here with all that commotion going on."

Both Max and I showed our commiseration.

Still smiling, Henry said, "Come with me." He led the way into the living room. He'd brought in a white outdoor bench from his swimming pool, as well as a white wicker chair. He waved us to the hard wooden bench. "I'm sorry, but that's all I have for my guests."

"It's all right," Max said, standing uncertainly in the middle of the big room. The room was strangely full of echoes. It was high and white and lighted by one full wall of tall windows.

Henry looked at us with sparkling eyes. "God, what big devils you both are." He looked at me and said, "I remember from your letters you said you were tall, but my God, not this tall." He said to Max, "And you, I'd heard you were a big man too. What did you guys eat when young?"

Max was a big man all right. He had heavy shoulders, big elbows, thick thighs, big knees. He was wearing a pair of sandals which did little to hide wide stubby feet. "It used to be such a burden. But with the new generation coming up with big fellows like Fred, it makes me feel better about it."

"Sit down."

We sat down together on the hard white bench. Henry sat down in the wicker chair across from us.

Henry looked at his hands with a self-amused smile. "I don't know what I did wrong with her. I thought we were getting along just great. But then like I said, all of a sudden she announced yesterday morning she was leaving. She called up the movers, and by evening she and the furniture and the kids were gone."

"You mean," Max said, "you were here watching it all go?"

"Yes. She left me the house, thank God, and my water colors." Henry nodded at several more gaudy prints hanging on the walls.

"Did she tell you why?" Max asked. Max shifted his huge bulk beside me sympathetically.

"No. Not a word. She just upped and left."

I could sense that Max was thinking the same thing I was, that maybe Henry couldn't make it with her in bed any more.

Henry said, "About a month ago I'd asked her if she needed a young stud to help take care of such needs as I couldn't." He smiled off to one side. " 'No,' she said then, 'no. You're too much for me as it is. And what makes it rough is that you're so old with it.' "

Max nodded.

"Lord, Max, well, here you are at last, in my own home," Henry said. "All my life I've been wanting to meet you. When you wrote your *Enjoyment of Laughter* I had to meet you. And when you were writing for the *New Masses* I had to meet you. But somehow it just never came about."

"Same here," Max said. "And thanks to our friend Fred here, it's finally happened."

"What are you doing at the Foundation?" Henry asked.

"Finishing the final draft of my autobiography."

"That I've got to read."

They talked about life in and around New York. Henry told about the days when he was a boss at Western Union, about all the funny situations he'd gotten into at times.

Talk got around to the famous fight between Max and Ernest Hemingway in Maxwell Perkins' office.

Max's explanation was a simple one. He spoke without rancor, without raising his voice. "Poor Ernest. I'd made some kind of remark in one of my pieces somewhere, teasingly, wondering if he really had hair on his chest. He took offense. I was in Perkins' office over at Scribners when he happened to come in. Ernest turned black when he spotted me, and without a word went for me. Well, I wasn't going to box with him. I didn't want him to hurt me, nor me hurt him. We were both writers. So I just wrapped my arms around him and we fell to the floor and we grunted and wrestled around a while and that was about all. Ernest couldn't do anything and I didn't want to. Perkins watched it all from behind his desk and after a while he suggested we stop it. We did. Ernest left in a huff without a word. Later on, Ernest, thinking his honor was at stake, issued a statement as to what had really happened in Perkins' office. If he'd have shut up nobody would have known about it. He blew the thing up all out of proportion. It was almost as if he were making up a fresh story. I decided to ignore it. Ernest is a good writer. Better than me."

Henry and Max talked about their various wives, why their marriages had failed. They seemed to agree that their wives had expected them to operate like bankers or merchants. The wives couldn't understand that a writer first writes because of something he's found and wants to get it down as true as he can, and then tries to sell it. Not the other way around. They discussed the various sex appetites of their wives. It was almost done apologetically, as if it were done more to share information than to share gossip. Henry didn't say much about his first wife with whom he'd had a lot of trouble. But he was full of praise for his second and third wives. The last two seemed to understand, a little, what it meant for him to be the artist, but they also wanted more a sense of security as to where the money to live on was coming from. He said he thought women were much more practical-minded, more down-to-earth, about the business of living than men.

I interjected, "What about women artists and their practical down-to-earth merchant husbands?"

Henry and Max smiled, nodded, and said I had a point.

Max thought his present young wife understood him. She was a good one.

"You're lucky," Henry said.

"What are you going to do now?" Max asked.

Henry smiled to one side. "Oh, slowly fill the house again with a few pieces of furniture and start over."

"You mean, have another wife?"

"Why not? I still enjoy love. I'm as good as I ever was."

Max looked at him quizzically.

"It's true," Henry said. "You should see the kinds of women who try to push in here. All the way from those just nubile to those in their eighties."

Max nodded. "Yes, I know what you mean." Then with a chuckle, Max added, "I used to say when I was in my fifties that I was looking for a girl with a father complex. But now I say I'm looking for a girl with a grandfather complex."

All three of us laughed. It was all wonderful male talk.

I wondered though to myself what sort of female talk Katherine Anne Porter, Caroline Gordon, and, say, Jean Stafford, could have were they to have a gabfest in a similar situation. I'd heard stories that Katherine Anne was a pretty lively old gal.

They talked about young writers coming up.

"The best is yet ahead for this country," Henry said. "The young are beginning to rebel against the old bucks running the show. The more rebellious the better."

Max agreed. "There is a new ferment going on in this country all right. One of strong dissent. And it can't help but be for the better."

Often the two old boars became so lost in their reminiscing, in comparing notes about the old days, they forgot I was present. Then, catching themselves, they'd turn to me to ask me something.

"Don't pay any attention to me," I said. "I'm having a good time just listening."

Max said, brows wrinkling, "But originally this was supposed to be your date with Henry."

I waved them back to their ruminations. "It wouldn't have been as good as this visit."

Finally it was time to go. Max had to catch his plane. Both Henry and Max got to their feet. A rueful, even sad, look came over their faces. They had to cut short what had been a great time. They stood facing each other a moment; and then, both at the same time, they stepped forward and gave each other a big hug.

I had to turn away a second.

Not once had they discussed what there was in it for them in the way of money.

I've also had talks with Robert Bly, Phil Dacey, James Gray, Donald Hall, Bill Holm, John Hassler, Madison Jones, Elmer Kelton, Herbert Krause, Andrew Lytle, David Madden, Thomas McGrath, John R. Milton, Marion Montgomery, Joe Paddock, J. F. Powers, Russell Roth, Jack Schaeffer, Wallace Stegner, Alan Swallow, Allen Tate, William Carlos Williams, James Wright. All of them in word and deed were "gentle men" with piercing minds. All of them were as eager as wonder-filled children to share such beauty and truth as they'd found—and they wanted to do it despite all opposition. All of them were true ministers of light. It was also true of women writers I've met (besides Meridel Le Sueur) : Dagmar Doneghy Beach, Carol Bly, Florence Dacey, Kathleen Hoagland, Caroline Marshall, Dorothy Johnson, Nancy Paddock, Martha Osten.so, Mari Sandoz, and my two poet daughters, Freya and Marya. All of them were bright inventive "gentle women."

I think the bad press the artist gets comes from bright men and bright women who, lamentably, find that they have no talent. They know they are bright, they are very good at taking things apart, even sometimes at putting things together, but they also know that they have no gift at making the things in the first place. All their lives they wonder why it is that John Swive and Susan Cope are able to write novels while they can't. They realize that John Swive and Susan Cope probably aren't much brighter than they are, but they can't figure out where that extra fillip comes from. So they check closely into the private lives of John Swive and Susan Cope, looking for the possible quirk, or kink, or flaw, that makes them different. Did John Swive's mother try to seduce him when she was giving him a bath as a boy? Did Susan Cope's father try to copulate with her the night she crept into bed with him during a storm (while mother was away)? Or, did John Swive's father kick him in the testicles in a fit of rage? Or, did Susan Cope's mother call her a whore? So that from then on John Swive and Susan Cope had to compensate for those traumatic experiences? Or, did a grain of sand somehow get lodged in their brainpans and like the clam, because of irritation, produce a pearl of wisdom? Those gems that flow out of John Swive's and Susan Cope's brains had to come from some unnatural source, one that, alas and alack, they the critics did not have?

Well, of course, if one looks long enough one can find fault with an Einstein, or a Gandhi, or a Jesus Christ; or even, for that matter, God Himself.

To repeat, it is difficult for me to believe that my presence brought out the best in those writers I've met, that my presence caused them to hide their worst. I know there are shadows in all men and all women. Not only are The Darks around us, they are in us. That is our common human lot. But the artist does not have a corner on that market.

It is my observation that, finally, the whole fully matured man is the strong man who has retained a kindly sensitivity. If our species is progressing toward some kind of ideal man and woman at all, it is toward some form of artist man and artist woman. He or she will be the harmonious person, at peace with himself or herself, forgiving of faults, kindly to the weak, eager in his or her makings to explore the unknown. The creative person tends to delve into what he or she finds in their "place," and then to dream from there. A productive artist can't help but be the loving person.

Without the artist we'd all still be pigs. Or at best hardly further advanced than the chimps in Africa. Without the artist there'd be no language, no tools, no face-to-face love-making, no wheel, no books, no spaceships. Without the artist such minds as C. G. Jung, Otto Rank, Harry Stack Sullivan would never have had the chance to elaborate on the concept that the ideal man has a beautiful soul in a beautiful body.

Even if we were to mix all of Mr. Sheed's findings in with my findings, that the artist is "wretch and rat" as well as "the true child of God," the artist still comes off pretty well. He is as human as the rest of us; and very probably can be compared to the best of us: Leonardo da Vinci, Jefferson, Einstein.

The artist is pretty much like everybody else — except that he or she has just a trace more of it.

February 8, 1973
At Blue Mound
January 11, 1983
At Roundwind

SCRAP BOOK

Report from Minnesota
Introducing Hubert Horatio Humphrey*

THE POLITICAL POT IS BOILING THESE DAYS IN MINNESOTA. This state, which has always been pretty independent in political matters, can furnish some interesting clues to the general situation in the Middle West and may give a hint or two in regard to the 1944 election.

The most interesting new political figure in Minnesota is a defeated candidate. Although Hubert H. Humphrey lost in the recent mayoralty campaign in Minneapolis, he made a showing which definitely put him on the map. It was the more surprising because he has an English name, and is dark, in a state which prefers its politicians to be blonds of Scandinavian origin.

Humphrey, a former political science professor, who worked his way through college as a druggist, is wiry, slim, built on springs. He is a persuasive orator. In the mayoralty campaign, he started as an unknown and in six weeks he rolled up a vote of 55,000 against incumbent Mayor Kline's 60,000. That vote astounded everybody, because Humphrey had some really great obstacles to overcome: namely, he knew little about practical politics; he was running against a better-than-average mayor who had not had a chance in his one term to cause irritation, and who was, as Roosevelt is nationally, the community's leader during a war crisis; he had yet to

* Originally published in the October 11, 1943 issue of *The New Republic*.

117

convince, beyond the AFL's endorsement, the rank-and-file laborer that he was his leader; he lacked the support of the CIO (though he got it after the primaries).

But Humphrey electrified the city in short order. Speaking as fast as a car could get him from meeting to meeting, he averaged eight talks a day, besides all of his personal contacts.

When Kline, in a radio address released to the press before delivery, claimed that Humphrey had been introduced to labor by a racketeer, Humphrey charged into the Mayor's office, followed by excited newspapermen and photographers who had been tipped off by his campaign managers. Humphrey demanded an explanation, and when it was not satisfactory, a retraction. Kline was so stunned he made some inadvertent remarks which copy-hungry reporters caught on the first bounce. One of the remarks was very unfortunate (for him) because he admitted he had not yet read his own speech. The next day's papers gave Humphrey an unprecedented and favorable amount of space. Humphrey wanted, and got, the campaign to move along progressive, educational lines.

Humphrey right now, with the salt of defeat in his system, is an important man in the state of Minnesota. Since Olson's death, the liberal cause in Minnesota, except for the Roosevelt majority in '40, has been languishing. The more callous say it has died. Political writers and dopesters have been saying that since 1938 when shrewd Harold E. Stassen was elected Governor, the back of the liberals, the Farmer-Labor Party, was broken — broken by a Republican machine modernized by liberal spicing. The writers have a point. Stassen's liberal talk (his conservative actions have been unheralded) resulted in the landslides of '38, '40 and '42.

These defeats have not been so much at the hands of a Republican hero, for Stassen is too calculating to make a voter feel warmly about him, as because of the fact that the liberals lack leadership.

The state Democratic Party has long been split because its leaders have been solely interested in dividing the patronage that comes from Washington and in grabbing a plum or two from either the Farmer-Labor or Republican Party, depending on which of the two offered more. And the Farmer-Labor Party is torn from within by the Benson and Peterson factions.

Roosevelt barely won in '40. If he runs in '44, he may lose — unless, all slippery factors remaining equal, the national Democratic heads pay some attention to the state. The Democrats must select a fiery local leader. If Olson were alive today, it would be a cinch. But he is gone. Humphrey is the one possibility.

The situation is serious. The press has been picking up the minor domestic errors of the Roosevelt administration. It has hammered on the Lewis imbroglio, the Office of Price Administration omissions and commissions, inflation threats, the recent oil scandals. And thus, since the liberals do not have the power to disseminate news through the press and the radio, they need vibrant leadership to match the reactionary attacks, particularly if Willkie gets the Republican nomination — and if he does, the liberal-tinted press will really go to town.

Actually, despite the press, the grumblings of housewives, the grousing of a few merchants, and the black markets, the labor unions in the state want the OPA to work. Many of them remember vividly how their fat wages melted away in the presence of the hot, high prices of the last World War. And the majority of the farmers, the renters and the farm-owners who have mortgages, which together comprise about 60 percent of the total, want stable prices. They know from concrete experience how the blown-up give-and-take of the last war's market put them in the renter-mortgagee class.

And the farmers want the subsidy plan, despite the stories in the press against it — further evidence that the Farm Bureau is not a truly representative organization. In rural Hennepin County, for example, where conservative farmers have twice elected Republican Gale to the House, there is considerable resentment now because he voted against the plan.

The state's 187,000 trade unionists are, of course, against the Smith-Connally law — and against the Minnesotans in Congress who voted for it (and most of them did) and who acted to override the President's veto. In the eyes of these voters, Roosevelt emerged a hero. And the meatless, queazy apologies that found their way into the editorial columns of the state's newspapers have made many a farmer wonder about the merits of the law. They're wondering if it's wise to jail the only crew that can work in the nation's mines.

The race riots in Detroit made the state shiver. It could have happened here. For though there aren't very many Negroes in Minnesota, and though one war-plant manager has mixed Negro workers with white workers successfully, there is a racial question here. It started violently in '38 when the reactionaries in hoarse whispers claimed that the Jews and the racketeers were running Governor Benson. Since then, not a campaign has come along without some vicious whispering. It was astounding to observe how even some of the local labor leaders wanted Humphrey to say, as a vote-getting technique, that Kline was being run by the Jews, that Kline was probably a Jew himself.

Though the racial question will be a problem for a long time to come, the isolationist sentiment has been pretty well dispersed. Even Hjalmar Peterson, the latest Farmer-Labor candidate for Governor and a rutabaga grower from Askov, Minnesota, is now plumping regularly in his weekly's editorial columns for the successful prosecution of the war. A wave of the hand must be given, too, to the press and to some of the Republican leaders: ex-Governor Stassen (now serving the country in a navy uniform), who has become nationally known for his program of war aims and his proposals for post-war coöperation with the nations of the world; Senator Ball, who was the first locally prominent politician to support Roosevelt's foreign policy, and was willing to campaign on it; and certainly eloquent Representative Judd, the former missionary to China.

Though Minnesota is geographically the most remote from enemy airfields, there is really a solid, cohesive movement to win the war as soon as possible and to win it right. Every Townsend Club, American Legion or Veterans of Foreign Wars meeting, whether it is local, district or statewide, refers constantly, by action and resolution, to post-war coöperation. And the whole state, labor, business, farm and church, has worked together to make the civilian-defense set-up effective.

Summer, 1943
In the Twin Cities

On Being a Western American Writer*

THE MAN WHO STANDS BEFORE YOU AT THIS MOMENT is someone who once was asked to take some state exams, in history, spelling, and so on, when he was about to graduate from the eighth grade at Doon, Iowa. His teacher was sure he'd sail through them all with near-hundreds right across the board. He did get near-hundreds — in everything except English, where he got 74, to his teacher's great astonishment, even shock. His general average was still high enough, though, for him to get a scholarship to go on to high school.

In high school I found myself in with students who were four or five years older than I. It was a parochial high school called Western Academy, at Hull, Iowa, and most of the students came from various outlying Dutch Calvinist communities. Many of them were boys who'd stayed home for three or four years after grade school to help their fathers on the farm and then finally one day had decided the farm wasn't for them. They'd got the call to either preach or teach in the Christian faith. So I found myself in competition, both intellectually and physically, with much older men, many of whom were quite bright and most of whom were certainly much more heavy and muscular than I. (I wasn't really very

* An extemporaneous speech given November 12, 1966, at Pullman, Washington, as part of a Symposium on the Historical Novel sponsored by the American Studies Group at the Washington State University.

122

big at twelve when I started high school.) The speech patterns of these older fellows were strange, to say the least, as most of them were raised in Dutch communities, while the rest of us were raised in American or worldly families or in Frisian families. (My family is of Frisian-Saxon descent.) At the same time, to complicate matters for me, my high school English teacher took quite a dislike to me mostly because I didn't do very well in English grammar. My marks in English just barely stayed above 75 all the way through. He told me later on after I'd got out of high school that the reason he'd finally passed me was that I always did very well in interpreting Shakespeare. We always had one day a week when we studied a play by Shakespeare, and I always did a very good job "reading" him. He said, "If I had to pass you on the grammar alone I'd have had to flunk you." Ha. Alan Swallow said this morning that it was difficult to flunk English. It wasn't for me.

I did get good marks in history, though, probably because my history teacher was really a novelist at heart. As he walked into the room to open the class, he'd spear somebody with a question that would rip you up like Dean Sonnichsen's question did me this morning, and right away the class was off and running. He did such a wonderful job of interpreting the ancient Greek society for me (I was thirteen years old then) that there are still times today when, as I'm driving along a certain road, or out walking, or looking at a certain configuration of nature, for a fleeting ripping second I'll have a picture of Athens, as if suddenly somebody has run three frames of a movie in front of me and then has snapped it off. I'll see the Parthenon gleaming, not in its present state, but the way it was in those old days, see people wearing tunics and, if it's a hot day, just a loincloth. I actually will smell, for a fleeting second, truly smell the leather thongs of their sandals thoroughly sweated through. I can pick that smell out because it's a different smell from ours. Yes, my history teacher was a magnificent teacher because he did a marvelous job of putting true images of those old days in my head. He almost made it a first-hand experience for me.

I finished high school, and my mother decided that I shouldn't go to college right away. I was the oldest son and so was eminently eligible to help my father on the farm. There was also some argument as to the value of further schooling, unless it was agreed I become either a minister or a teacher. I was by this time quite a hulking brute and all the relatives told my father that he was throwing away a very good hired man if he let me go on to school. I couldn't go on my own because the rule was, you see, that you didn't keep any money you might earn until you were twenty-one — your dad kept it. And he had to do this to make sure that the entire family survived. Further, my mother was a little worried about the fleshpots— even those of Calvin College in Grand Rapids, Michigan, a college run by the Dutch Calvinist churches in America. She felt I shouldn't have a chance to look at the fleshpots until I was at least eighteen.

So I stayed home for two years between high school and college. My mother was ailing and I felt I should listen to her. I had no sisters, just five younger brothers, so we were all asked to pitch in not only with the farm work but also the housework. But she died anyway. Staying home I fell into the habit of using the language around me more than ever, both at home and in town and on the farms around, "Siouxland language," as I call it, which is as distinct and as worthwhile as the vernacular that Mark Twain picked up in Hannibal, Missouri. At the same time I read a lot. When I could. I always was an omnivorous reader. At first my father was proud of my reading accomplishments because it was something he could never do. He hadn't gone to school much and couldn't read or write in those days. He was proud of me — until he discovered that the reading and writing were leading me away from him. He then tried to forbid it. So I read at night, under the blankets with a flashlight — until that was discovered. Then I read up in the hay-mow between chores. And I read on the plow once I was over the hill out of sight of the yard. During those two years I read all of Shakespeare and all of Jack London.

When I started college, I just wandered onto the campus with my high-water pants, not knowing much about anything and not knowing quite what to do. A senior spotted me adrift and it was he who laid out my program for me. He'd also got an earful of my vernacular and it was he who decided that I should take English from a spinster (whom for the moment we shall call Miss Censor). "You better have Miss Censor for your English teacher because she's the strictest and you'll learn some English from her." Apparently he didn't understand either that I spoke first-rate vernacular Ameri-can. So I found myself in the hands of this Miss Censor. It wasn't long and, boy, she and I were at crossed swords. She was unmar-ried, about thirty, wore military clothes, had a slight moustache, wore square-toed shoes, had a brisk sharp walk, had a deeper voice than I at the time — but knew her English. Well, around Christ-mas time the ax fell. I got all my themes back. I don't know why she'd waited that long to give it to me, but she did. As I paged through the themes I saw that they were getting bloodier and bloodier with red marks. Finally I got to the one that was supposed to be the big paper. I saw right away what had happened. She'd read two pages, filling them full of red marks; then got terribly dis-gusted and wrote at the bottom of the page: "Dear Mr. Feikema, Why can you not [not, why can't you] use better English? I'm sorry, but this will never do at all. Miss Censor." When I got all my marks at the end of the semester, there was an F for English.

Earlier in the semester the basketball coach at Calvin had seen me walking around on the campus a few times and it gradually dawned on him that he might make a basketball player out of this pair of highpockets. I was pressed into the ranks, made to play basketball. If I played basketball I could get a job on the campus and so continue my way through school. I didn't do too badly at freshman basketball (I'd played some baseball as a boy), so you can imagine what happened when the coach saw that F. He turned hail-white. All the big games were coming up for the frosh squad. There were some quick faculty meetings over this matter of the Feikema F. They discovered that I'd gotten C's and C-pluses in most of my other courses, with even a B-plus in Bible Study. Of course that B-plus in Bible looked very good. What they didn't know though was that at home, since my father couldn't read or write, I'd read the Bible at family service from the age of eight on, morning, noon, and night. By the time I'd arrived at Calvin I'd read the Bible through seven times, including the begats. I knew the Bible better than the professor there. And, I'd read it in Dutch, and I'd read it in English, and I'd heard it recited in Frisian — three different versions — so I even had a somewhat comparative knowledge of the Bible. Well, it was finally decided, with Miss Censor getting down on her knees by her bed as to the morality of what the faculty planned, that I would be given "a conditional mark of some sort," that if I did much better work in the second semester she was to pass me for both semesters.

I wanted to go home when I saw that F. In fact, I was packed and ready to go, when one of the boys upstairs spotted me. He'd been one of those who'd laughed a little at my attempts at violin playing but now he was concerned. (If someone ridicules you a little he's really betraying the fact that behind it all he sort of likes you — he doesn't quite like you the way you are but he does like you after a fashion.) He took me out for a long walk. He fed me some glazed doughnuts which he knew I loved. I actually wept.

A lot. And I don't cry very easy. Except when reading letters from girl friends. I was very lonesome and homesick for Iowa. I thought Grand Rapids, Michigan, the worst place on earth. For a little while. But finally my new friend talked me into staying.

I still had left this terrible problem with Miss Censor. I tried to switch out of her class, but this of course she wouldn't permit at all. This was absolutely against her principles. So I had to bull it through somehow. And the Lord knows I tried. I tried everything I could think of to learn what it was she wanted out of me. Why were these themes of mine failures all the time?

Well, the way I got around it went back to something I'd learned on the farm. When you want to learn how to pick corn, for example, you ape the best cornpicker around. I aped my dad. Instead of the way you might think to pick an ear, you do it this way — hook attached to the palm of your hand, you pull the hook through the husks around the ear, like this, so that the corn ear falls into your fingers, like this, and then you simply throw the ear against the bangboard, from where it falls into the wagon. And you do it all in one motion. Not two motions. One. So I decided that the best way for me to learn how to write themes for Miss Censor was to listen to her very intently in class, not to the content of her talk, but to the style of her talk. To the way she said everything. Then, with that in my head, and buzzing inside with her manner, I'd rush home to my room in the dorm and I'd write the theme assigned for the next class in her rhythms, her accents, her language. And . . . by the Lord I did so well at aping her that she gave me a retroactive C for the first semester and a B-minus for the second semester.

My adventures with the English department at Calvin continued (with a professor who for the moment we'll call Professor Ban). Professor Ban was one of the best readers of poetry I've ever heard, better even than Allen Tate or T. S. Eliot; but as a teacher he wasn't too good. The first semester I worked like a dog in his Shakespeare course. I thought I knew it almost as well as he. I wrote a very fine paper on Shakespeare. Well, I got a B-plus. No more. Several of the girls got A's. So the next semester I loafed all the way through his course in Victorian Literature. Didn't do a tap of work. B-plus. He had me pegged for B-plus and that was it. I met him again seven years ago at a class reunion. By that time, of course, it'd become known that I'd written a few books. He was a very old man by then, though hearty, and on his umpteenth wife, and he comes up to me, and he says in his East Anglia accent, which I can't imitate, "Mr. Feikema, Manfred, why didn't you tell me you wanted to be a novelist? I would have spent some time with you in college." Ah, well, afterthoughts, afterthoughts.

Somewhere in college, though, I finally did work out what had been going on. It had something to do with the difference between Mark Twain and Henry James. Both are Americans and both present quite different American faces. And I was a Mark Twain man. Mark Twain was at his best when he used Western vernacular, middle Mississippi River vernacular. Both Miss Censor and Professor Ban had tried to make me over into a Henry James man. But in truth I was a Mark Twain man. It took some while for me to understand that my natural tongue, the language I talked back home in Siouxland, was not English but something else. It was English-American. A different language.

This understanding has become very important to this someone who lives west of the Mississippi and who writes about the Midlands and the Far West. It is my conviction that a new language is being created out here west of the Mississippi. We've given up on a modern England English, on an English that is polysyllabic, often heavy, a governmentese kind of English, an English don English, and no longer an English rooted in Chaucer. The modern England

English has certainly drifted radically away from the English used by such a writer as Charles Montagu Doughty. (No one here has probably ever heard of Charles Montagu Doughty. Have you? Doughty lived a century ago and tried to reroute and reroot the language of his day back to the language of Chaucer and Spenser. He eschewed Shakespeare. He wrote a magnificent travel book in this language of his called *Travels in Arabia Deserta*, and many epic poems, one of them six volumes long called *Dawn in Britain*. Shaw said of Doughty, by the way, in his afterword to the Galaxy edition of his own *Back to Methuselah*: "There must have been something majestic and gigantic about the man that made him classic in himself . . . and when he came home (from Arabia) he spent the rest of his life in writing immense prophetic epics in blank verse of a Himalayan magnificence and natural eminence that would have made a Milton gasp.")

I think that what the Western American writer is doing out here (I know I am) is something as follows. He is first of all making it a point to hang onto all the old basic Anglo-Saxon words, such words as "stone," "floor," "tree," "oat," and the like. (In the Frisian language the word for "floor" is *floer*, and the word for "stone" is *stien*, and the word for "summer" is *simmer*, so you see as an American of Frisian descent it comes naturally for me to hang onto such simple Anglo-Saxon words. I might tell you, by the way, that the Frisians had a wonderful shibboleth which they used in ancient days to find out if you were a fifth column spy. They'd ask a Hollander trying to sneak into Friesland to repeat the following after them: *Buter, brea, en griene tsiis, hwa thet net sizze kin is gjin oprjochte Fries*. Which translated means: "Butter, bread, and green cheese, who that cannot say is not an upright (or true) Fries." The Hollander pretending he was a Frisian could never properly pronounce the word *oprjochte*.

By the way, I should tell you that in the little exposure to Chaucer I had in college I discovered to my great astonishment that I could read him. I readily knew about two-thirds of Chaucer because I'd heard Frisian spoken as a boy. The only Chaucer words I didn't catch immediately were those horrible invasion words from Normandy. Words of French origin. The same sort of words our government clerks like to parade. As well as our scientists. I seem to be digressing, but the digressions are interesting, so I'm going to follow them for the moment. You see, every time you use a poly-syllabic word, especially one of Latin origin, you are placing a series of shields or walls between your meaning and your listener. Every prefix and every suffix is just another obstacle through which your listener must pierce to get at the meat of what you mean, get at the true core or root of the word — which core word or root word once had "hit" in its own right in its original usage back in Old Italy but which no longer has for us sitting as we do in the middle of our own mother tongue. Polysyllabic words tend to have learned mean-ings for us rather than natural meanings — natural meanings as such words as "stone" or "floor" have for us now. Originally for the Latin people the core of a polysyllabic word once had bite. But it no longer has for us. It is feelingless. Such a word as "bibliophile" is a long nice word, it sounds pretty elegant, it even sounds intelli-gent — but it doesn't have the hit or the bite of its Anglo-Saxon equivalent "book lover." To go back — the reason the Western American writer is hanging onto all the old hard Anglo-Saxon words is this: they work for him out here in the wilds and the open spaces.

Further, the Western American writer is also very busy replacing the dead polysyllabic words with modern American inventions. With slang. Now most slang is of little value. That's been true of any age and in any time. It isn't just our age in this country. But it is the good writer's impulse (and duty) to pick out those slang words that will have lasting hit and bite in them. It's like finding an agate in a gravel pit. Most pebbles are of little value except as something to step on. But every now and then you find a pebble that, with a little shining up and a little cleaning up, you can wear on your finger. When you find a word like that you set it up in your sentence so that it not only works but it shines. And if you have a keen ear, and a keen eye, it will probably last a long time just as the basic Anglo-Saxon words still do. Inventions like "bulldozer," "rattail file," "caterpillar tractor," "buckskin," "monkey wrench," "skyscraper," "wallow," "rawhide." A carpenter at work upstairs wanting a certain kind of file will call down to his helper, "Hey, kid, toss up the rattail file, will you?" The kid will right away know what he means. Because it's a file that looks like the tail of a rat and is used to ream out holes in wood, to widen them all around, say for a doorhandle.

I know that in my writing — and I think this is also true of Fisher's, Waters', and Clark's — I know that I am constantly on the alert for new words that will work in place of the dead words. I am often the victim of my more learned associates and so find myself using a polysyllabic word now and then in the first draft. But when I do use such a polysyllabic I'll replace it with an Americanism in the final draft. Sometimes I'll go all through the countryside and all through town (in my memory) to find a replacement if I don't like the dead word. And it's my hope that by this process I'll be using a language that will be as alive a hundred years from now as Mark Twain's language is for us today.

Language never stands still. If a people have generations a language will have generations. Dante wrote his *The Divine Comedy* in what was considered a vernacular, even regional, language by the grammarian perfectionists of his day. But Dante's book won out because not only was the concept brilliant but the usage of the vernacular was consistent and all of a piece. And where are those perfectionist academes of his time today?

The language that Chaucer worked out in his day, and Shakespeare in his day, were languages that worked for the time and the place and the people, all three. It came out of their ethos, the *in situ*, the way things were at the time. (Look at the charge Shakespeare puts into his plays. Sometimes he puts in real stretchers. *King Lear*, for example. Every now and then the play is interrupted by great thunderclaps, lightning and thunder. Well, now, any one who has read the meteorological history of England knows that that little island has probably only one thunderstorm a year, perhaps only one in ten years — certainly not like we have them here in America, out in the plains. And if he could take such liberties with his experience, why can't we with ours?)

Any echo of the aborigine in England is pretty well lost in the English language as used today in England. Whereas in our language the echo and the feel and even some of the talk of the aborigine is still in our American language. Because it works. Because it reflects our experience. It reflects not an English experience but an American experience. You know, if you sit long enough next to a swamp and if you're bitten a thousand times by a mosquito and if you finally don't exclaim, "Goddam those mosquitoes!" there's something wrong with you. An environment is going to make you bend your language. It is bound to make it bend. The English never see violently twisting windstorms in England. (Their sailors may see waterspouts out at sea.) But we do. Very often in the summer. So we invented the word "tornado" to describe it. We had to save our lives in some instances. (We like to think sometimes that our American history is a long and noble one. But measured against the history of the English tongue which goes back beyond even Sanskrit times it is but a short one. So with our language changing dynamically as fast as it is it may very well be that six hundred years from now our novels may be as hard to read for the average student of that future time as Chaucer is for the student of today.)

In the beginning the English language didn't change too fast when the Pilgrims brought it over. The first push and shove into this new land was done so furiously that the Englishman erased much aborigine lore. Also the weather and life generally in the Eastern part of America is much milder than it is out here. All storm systems come off the Pacific and by the time they reach the Eastern seaboard they are pretty well leeched out, have become pretty weak and effeminate. So that there was some reason for preserving the English language as she was out on the east coast. But as the language moved first South and then West, it underwent a violent transformation, albeit a natural one. The swamps and the mountains, the heat and the cold, the rainstorms and the snowstorms (or as we Western Americans say now, "the cloudbursts and the blizzards"), the grasslands and the deserts, all these new things, were something the users of the English language had to somehow describe and, if possible, accept. And this is what the Western American writer is doing more than any other American writer.

It's as though a place finds its voice through whatever creatures happen to live in that place, rooted or footed, trees or people moving about; as though a place shapes a people and then shapes the language they use. We are all really in the grip of something greater than we imagine or realize, not only you as readers but we as writers. We all can't help but be shaped by the place in which we live. This is something that the Eastern critic and the Eastern scholar and the Eastern reviewer and the Eastern editor can't get through his head. He keeps thinking we should talk and write like he does. He's as bad as my Miss Censor in college was. And if they must attack us, jump on our backs, be personal about it, why don't they, if they want to be effective about it, attack the thing, our place, that's got us in its grip? (Actually they don't mind us personally so much as that they are irritated by the primordial voice that is still alive in the American land and that still speaks through us. We are more rooted into the nature of things than they are and this they resent. By comparison they are rootless.)

When I was doing my first seven novels, under the old name of Feike Feikema, I was aware of the fact that my place was not getting its full voice, its full say, expressed through me. All artists have a feeling of inadequacy, for one reason or another. But I knew what part of mine was. I wasn't getting quite the timbre or resonance in my things that say a Hardy got into his work. (Apart from talent.) Hardy not only reflected his times but also reflected a long cultural history before that. Every time Hardy made a move on paper twenty wonderful writers behind him in time were also making a move on paper, giving him part of their wiggles. Place had shaped Chaucer and Spenser and Shakespeare and Milton and finally a Hardy, so that they all wrote in what we call a tradition, and achieved a cultural momentum *in a given country*. But I couldn't very well use their place-dictated language and tradition. My place called for something different.

I began to look into the past of my place. I decided that the first place to start with would be with my grandfathers and my great uncles. As a boy I'd often heard them talk about pioneer times. (Ha. To get them to open up I sometimes had to give them homebrew beer. They didn't care much for the tepid 3.2 beer of the day. They had their own recipes for beer, a beer, by the way, which was so pure that it rarely had any settlings in it. My dad's beer popped like champagne when you opened a bottle, with a little smoke coming off of it. Sometimes a neighbor would be in a hurry to have beer and would bottle it green. Then you had to hold it into a cream can when you uncapped it to keep it from blowing foam all over the place.) They told how it felt as a white people to be moving in and pushing out the Yankton Indians.

Inquiring further I discovered that they'd been preceded by the trappers who made it a point to get along with the Indians, sometimes even marrying into an Indian family. I got this information from an old trapper, who, when he had a little too much beer, would tell you everything. It was these trappers, I learned, who gave most of the names we now have for places — both American names as well as Indian names.

Well, who was there before the trappers? The Yankton Indians, as mentioned. So I visited some of the old chiefs on the reservations. And got their story. (I might mention I spent ten years getting ready to write *Lord Grizzly*. I ran across the Hugh Glass story while writing *This Is the Year*. It kept coming back to me as I wrote the trilogy *Wanderlust*. Kept coming back. It caught up many of the things I was looking for back in those old times. It began from a fragment and kept growing in my mind.) (You know, big things don't happen to you in a big way, like, say, a visitation from above such as Saint Paul experienced on the road to Damascus. The big things start in a little way. First there's a tiny bing, and then there's a silence, and then there's another tiny bing, sometimes a couple of them, and then there's another silence — but finally when you get a series of mmmmmmmm quick bings, well, then you know something is going on there in the back of your head and you'd better pay attention to it.)

And who was there before the Yankton Sioux? Well, there I had to dig into anthropology. And doing so I discovered that the whole American anthropological world was in somewhat of an up-

roar, that they were divided into two schools of thought in somewhat of the same manner as American literature today is. The old-
line Eastern anthropologist, the Hootens and the Hrdličkas, tried to
denigrate (ha!, there's another one of those dummed polysyllabic
words), run down Indian history, saying that they'd only recently
come to America, like the white man himself, and so therefore it
wasn't such an awful thing for the superior white people to throw
out the inferior red people. But the newer Western anthropologist
had a different story. And his story was based on the increasing
number of artifacts he was finding. That the Indian had been on
this continent for say, six, seven, even thirty, forty thousand years.
That he hadn't necessarily come by way of the Bering Straits, that
he might have even come by way of the South Pacific when that
ocean was some four hundred feet lower due to one-time huge polar
icecaps, come island-hopping. That as a matter of fact, a road being
a road, it can be traveled both ways, so that the birthplace of man
may not be in Africa after all, but possibly in one of the most beautiful spots on earth, the Amazon river basin. (By the way, I once saw
a colored slide of a small green jade jaguar that was found in a sedi-
ment deposit laid down ten thousand years ago in the Amazon river
basin. It had a Maltese Cross cut into it. Now how did that Maltese
Cross get over there when it is supposed to have come from the
island of Malta in fairly modern times?) In any case, all this new
anthropological lore was most exciting. Suddenly you realized that
the land you lived in had a great and an ancient history of its own—
and that this history was vitally alive!

And who was here before the man who lived here forty thousand
years ago? Dinosaurs and mastodons.

And before them? Small creatures. Squirrels and little three-
toed horses. (By the way, the horse is believed to have originated in
America, and then to have moved on to Asia and then to Europe.

If the first horse could have taken that route west across the Bering Straits, then the first man could possibly have taken that route too.)

And who before them? Lichen.

And who before that? Algae in water.

And who before that? The sun itself. Finally.

To sum it all up: It has become my impulse and my duty to become a voice for all these things.

Sometimes when things go bad for me in the publishing world, and I fight with my wife about why it is I don't earn more money, I remember my friends, the pioneers and the trappers and the Indians and the dinosaurs and the little three-toed horses and the lichen and the algae and the great sun itself, and I say to myself in this moment of discouragement: "Wait a minute. This is important, this glimpse of a place and of a literature you have. You have this knowledge now. You can't back away from it. You've got to put her down. Frangible and fragile as it all may be, you've got to put her down."

So we're here now. We have these skies. We have these trees. We have this basalt here outside this building. And we're setting up our little nuclei of cultures across these plains and up into the mountains. Our culture is already of a high order and yet we're still not too crowded. We have a very good chance of doing something great out here which they no longer have in that vast megalopolis that exists in Eastern America. That continuous city in the East, which starts below Washington, D. C., and goes all the way to Boston and then around to Cleveland and Detroit and then by way of Pittsburgh back to Washington, D. C., again, has become too big to have any cultural future, to produce creative geniuses. That great sea of mud, social mud, will drown all talent. Too big. The greatest explosion of genius that ever occurred came about in a Greece with a population of less than a hundred twenty-five thousand.

Not so long ago a psychologist who was pondering this same problem of too many in too small a place did an experiment with rats. First he put a certain number of rats in a certain sized place at about the same ratio they might comfortably have under a corn-crib. He fed them well and watched them. He observed that so long as he kept their number down to a certain limit they seemed happy together. But the moment he allowed them to overpopulate things began to happen. Especially to the males. A good many of the males became docile. Some acted like females. Some died strange quiet deaths. If the population still continued to rise, the offspring began to die before maturity. Finally even some of the females began to act like neuters. The whole rat community began to act nervous and irascible. The usual behavioral lines became muddy. Finally, to complete the experiment, he depopulated the rat community, brought it down numerically to its former state when things were happier. Immediately all the males became frisky and hearty again and the females went back to their old roles of nest building. The whole community bustled with its old time vitality.

I don't know what you're going to do with that overpopulated East. They're there now. And I like them all personally when I meet them. We'll just have to sit and wait and see what happens.

But in the meantime they shouldn't point any fingers at us because the mud hasn't reached us yet, because we don't have enough culture out here according to their standards. Because the truth is we're the only ones left who have a chance to do something lasting for America.

Well, that's enough.

November 12, 1967
In Pullman, Washington

In Memoriam Address*
Sinclair Lewis, 1885–1951

IT IS A CUSTOM AMONGST THE CIVILIZED TO SPEAK A FEW WORDS
OVER THE GRAVES OF THE JUST DEAD. No matter what the departed
man or woman or child may have been in life, saint or sinner,
genius or dimwit, plutocrat or pauper, citizen or criminal, he or she
or it is usually accorded the ritual. In this instance we are here to
perform the ritual, the magic incantation so to speak, for a man who
was baptized Harry Sinclair Lewis and who was known to the world
as Sinclair Lewis and who was known to his friends as Red Lewis.

Red Lewis: born in Sauk Centre, Minnesota, USA. Deceased
in Rome, Italy, Europe.

Just to put it that way is to suggest immediately that we have
here something out of the ordinary, that we have a wanderer on our
hands, a world's wanderer even, a man who not only wanders
through the world but is possessed by the world. Looking back we
see that in his boyhood there was evidence that Red had wild heels
and a winged mind. He was restless from the beginning. He did
not fit the usual grooves that friends, neighbors, relatives lived in
around him. The first real sign of it was not so much his antics in
school or on the playgrounds but in the fact that he read books

---

* On the occasion of the burial of Sinclair Lewis' ashes in Sauk Centre,
Minnesota, Sunday, January 28, 1951.

omnivorously both in the home and in the library. Which is a way of saying that when restlessness, energy, becomes hitched to literacy, or, rather, when ideas are invested with vital force, something is likely to happen.

It did happen. It wasn't long before Red decided that he wanted to become a writer. This is not at all unnatural. Writing was one of the first arts to have been developed by the mind of man. It is also one of the most revered by man. The printed word, for most of mankind, is almost like the word of God. For some savages a few words written on a scrap of paper have more magic power than do towering hundred foot totem poles.

It has been argued by some discerning critics that writing did not come naturally to Red. And what we hear of his early days seems to confirm this. One of his first jobs was that of reporter for a Waterloo, Iowa, paper. After a couple of weeks of it his editor told him to forget it. He wasn't a writer. When Red handed in his first novel the publisher told him the same thing. Forget it, he wasn't a novelist. Red persisted. And still the difficulty seemed to remain — his next five novels, though published, were neither distinguished nor successful.

Yet, and this is the story, yet he continued to persist and on his seventh try he finally did it. Wrote the book *Main Street* which became world famous and which helped change the whole course of modern American literature, perhaps even world literature, a book which over the years sold over 2,000,000 copies in the United States alone, and that despite a spearing satire, a satire that robbed men of comforting fictions.

Does this prove then that Red was really a writer afterall? It can be argued: not necessarily. Because it can be argued that Red was not a natural and a fluent writer as say Scott Fitzgerald was. Red was a struggle writer. Well, what then of his fame as a writer?

Again it can be argued that we have here an example of how emotional force and mental brilliance lifted and developed an ordinary talent into greatness — something we also find in the case of his famous contemporary, Theodore Dreiser. Writing came hard for Red Lewis, he had to wrestle with it, and out of the wrestling came discipline and the need to work for the rest of his life. Writing came easy for Scott Fitzgerald and, one can argue, because of it Scott did not learn discipline. The greatest novelists in the world have all, in a sense, been average stylists. Dickens, Tolstoi, Balzac, Dumas, were all on occasion sloppy writers. They were not neat, precise, dainty. They did not let their own style possess them as it seems to have done in the case of, say, Hemingway. They had seen much, and had much to say, and had only sixty, sixty-five, seventy years to say it in.

Would Sinclair Lewis, then, have been greater had he chosen an art form more at home to him? say, musical composition? say, scientific inquiry? say, painting? Possibly. Or would Sinclair Lewis, then, have been greater in some genre not yet developed by the genius of mankind? Just possibly. Which leads us to the unhappy and frustrating thought: how many undeveloped Mozarts lived and died before Western Culture developed the form of the symphony? or, to put it on a more mundane level, how many unrealized Babe Ruths and Dizzy Deans lived and died before the game of baseball was invented? In any case, whether or not his original starting talent was of average or of above-average worth, Red used what he had like a genius to build against the assault of time itself.

Red Lewis died in Rome. Why Rome of all places?

Rome is the fountainhead of Western Culture; or, rather, it is the civilization that handed on the genius of other civilizations before it, the Greek, the Egyptian, the Babylonian, the Judean, the great Cretan, and countless unremembered ones. Why should Sinclair Lewis have wanted to spend his last days there? We'll probably never know. Perhaps he didn't know. But we can hazard a guess. Could it be that in his furious wandering and in his furious searching he finally got wind, got scent, of the real drift of humankind's living here on earth? that he was willynilly on the trail of: What does this living mean here? and so felt that he had to go search out this trail, now almost cold, with the first stop being Rome, the gateway into an even colder past? Was there in Red an instinctive reaching back to his and to Western Civilization's origins? Or, was it merely that as he aged he felt the need to live in an aged society? Or both? Or more?

It can also be argued that at the last of his life this furious burning in Red, this furious almost outraged force in him, carried him beyond mere literary greatness, made him go too fast too continuously, so that his later books became thin, not so much as some critics have put it because he had less and less to say but more that he was no longer in them, that he was beyond them like some human jetplane beyond its own sound. It is a likely argument. We know that another great writer named Leo Tolstoi raced beyond, went beyond, mere fiction writing, mere art production, to seek who-knows-not-what in the world beyond the writing-desk.

I did not know Red Lewis as well as many others did. My first knowledge of him was through one of his books. When I was a very young man in college I ran across his *Elmer Gantry*. It helped me make up my mind at the time not to go into the ministry, something that my dead mother had wanted very much. Actually, of course, I had already made up my mind not to become a minister. But the printed word did help me stick to the decision. Red's printed word was the magic charm for me. It was God's word for me at the time. Red's printed word did not tell me that the ministry was an undesirable profession. Not at all. The ministry is like any other honorable profession. It has its good points as well as its bad points, its good men as well as its bad men. No, it was rather that Red's printed word told me that if I went into the ministry feeling as I did about it at the time I would have become a bad minister, would have become the hypocrite he despised. Red's words told me to persist in the youthful and wonderful folly of believing in being an honest man — even if that meant being something other than a minister. In effect, then, Red saved the ministry from me.

Elmer Gantry led me to his other books: *Main Street, Babbitt, Arrowsmith, Dodsworth,* many of which I admired, in particular *Arrowsmith* in which it seemed to me he had his eye most clearly on that most difficult of human goals, where Truth is Beauty and as a result Beauty is Truth. Yes, I admired much of his work, though I must say honestly that I never considered them my particular models to follow or to imitate, no more than he considered the works of his literary uncles his particular models. But I did acknowledge the verity of his goals, and I did model myself after his general and his passionate pursuit of them. In that sense he was my friendly literary uncle — yes, even my father.

Later, I met him a few times, once spent a week with him in his home in Duluth. He was very kind to me. He had some advice to offer me as a young stripling in his field. He showed me how he gathered his notes, how he organized them, how he executed them. He warned me about the various pitfalls that lay ahead for me; in particular telling me how I should handle that seemingly necessary evil — the critics. As he talked, there was no air of patronizing. Rather he spoke as the good father would speak to his unknowing son.

Truth to tell, afterwards, I am sure, very sure, that he was not always pleased with what his son did. Just as, no doubt, his spiritual or literary father was not always pleased with what he had done. But Red Lewis was a wise father. He knew that each son and each daughter had to work out his or her own way, with as little interference from the old folks as possible. Red always insisted that the new generation coming in had to have its own freedoms and its own ways of living. The old folks could not live the lives of the young folks.

Much has been made of the fact that Red Lewis the man and Sinclair Lewis the artist were lonely. Much has also been made of the theory that the American artist is lonely in America.

In the case of Lewis we know he was lonely, incredibly lonely. He was so lonely in the beginning that he left his Minnesota home to seek the fleshpots of the cities in the East and in Europe; he was so lonely in his middle years that he came back to America and bought and sold more homes in various sections of America than is ordinarily permitted even the most privileged of men in this our accidentally most privileged of nations; he was so lonely in his last years that he consciously or unconsciously began to seek out his origins as a child of the Western Civilization by sojourning in its older cultures.

And Lewis *was* lonely. When you met him you instantly felt compassion for him. Not because he lacked vigor or strength or selfhelp, but because he had too much of these things. His eyes, his face, his hands, all seemed to cry for affection, for simple love between men and men. And when you smiled at him, or indicated that you had some sense of his worth to you both as friend and as artist, he almost broke his back, yea, gave the shirt off his back even, to be good to you.

Up to a point. Because it wasn't long before Lewis' natural wary instincts warned him he might be endangering both himself and his livelihood by keeping his hand open too long. He knew history, that it is full of instances of betrayal, where Joseph's brothers turn on Joseph, where Saul turns on David, where Judas turns on Christ, where Sparta turns on Athens, where Brutus turns on Caesar, where Anthony turns on still another Caesar, where, in Lewis's own field, a friend turns on Edgar Allen Poe and forever leaves a blight on Poe's great fair name, where, in the realm of human brotherhood, Englishman and Russian and American and Spaniard and Frenchman and Italian, turn on each other with bared and knife-sharp teeth of destruction. Red Lewis knew.

It is the old story of everybody wanting to be the king — except the king. Men create kings. Either passively or actively. We are all brothers, yes. But we are more. Living apart and separate in this fragile sack of skin, we are insecure, both as individuals and as brothers. And, in addition, we are all busy making a living, getting a subsistence at least, keeping the sack of skin hale and hearty if possible. And these two, insecurity and hunger, cause us, first to need, and then to hope, and then to seek a Something or a Someone who will Save Us, as we say, who will Protect Us, who will Love Us. And since there is no more obvious a combination of both Power and Mind known to man than what man finds in himself, man exalts these two aspects of himself and attributes these exalted aspects to some one man and makes him King. Some people choose kings by breeding, some by lot, some by vote. In any case, King someone has to be and King someone is.

Some men, because of the heredity handed down to them, either by their father's hand or by their father's genes, have more energy, or more mental excellence, or more will power, or better organization of their parts — whatever it is — and it is these upon whom the bloodbirth, the lot, the vote falls. The Call to Kingship comes. And off they must go to live beneath the Golden Bough.

It is no accident that Christ was and still is called both the Son of Man and the Son of God. And it is no accident either that we are not afraid of that part of Christ which we call the Son of Man and that we fear that part of him which we call the Son of God: Thus it is that He must be of us as well as apart from us — at the same time.

Men not only need this kingship, they also use it. Because it is power: power to bring food, power to get clothing, power to provide shelter, power to acquire comfort, yes, even power to obtain second-rate kingships. Thus men seek the favor of the King, not so much because they love him as the Son of Man, which they may, but more because they need him as the Son of God.

Now he who has been chosen to be the Son of God as well as the Son of Man, knows this, knows that they seek help from the image that they have read into him. And Sinclair Lewis as the artist king knew this. And Sinclair Lewis as the world artist king, not just the American artist king, knew this.

The American artist isn't the only lonely artist king. Artists, writers, have been lonely the world over, have been lonely in every culture known to man. Can you name one great artist who felt at home in his culture? Homer? Read Plato's notion of what the artist should mean to his society. Virgil? Read his *Georgics.* Dante? Read his homesick laments. Goethe? Read his *Faust.* Cervantes? Read his *Don Quixote.* Camoens? Read his *The Lusiad.* Shakespeare? Read *Hamlet* or *King Lear.* Tolstoi? Read the tracts he wrote after he quit writing novels. Mann? Read *Der Zauberberg.* As artists, as kings, they have all been homesick for a home. And it is with pity that one looks at the Expatriates who think they have to go to the Left Bank in Gay Paree, or to Eternal Rome, to find their home — where they meet Parisian artists or Roman artists who have to go to America now to find their "home."

Home for the artist? Never.

But, and ah! this is it — is there a home for the Son of Man in man? Possibly. Just possibly. And it is this part of the King, the Son of Man, who should stay, if possible, near the place of his birth, near his fleshly roots. Because then at least a part of the King's ravenous hunger will be appeased. Which may keep him from becoming a despot. Which may give us a chance as neighbors to see that he remains "safe for us."

It is to the eternal credit of the manhood, and of the artist, in Sinclair Lewis that he tried, most of his life, to live in the country he was born in.

We stand here, then, looking down upon the still warm ashes of this brave and once eager warrior, this once powerful greatheart. We speak the words. And as we speak, we know that lofty words will not bring Red Lewis back, nor increase by a whit the height of his stature as a man, nor bring him a step nearer heaven, nor endear him the more in the eyes of a God in heaven. Lofty words will not touch him, nor change him, nor gladden him. He is now insensitive to anything we might do for him, or say of him, or demand of him. Mortal concerns are all out of his hands.

His course is run. His log is written. And it needs only the work of reading the log to know how well or how poorly he captained his craft across life's serene seas and tumultuous oceans.

What we have left, then, is us, and our sense of loss. Thus, really, we are addressing ourselves.

We speak because we must speak to each other. We speak for *our* comfort, not his. Looking down at these his warm ashes it is as if we are reaching ahead to realize our own deaths, What will It be like? now while we are still alive, as if, to make our deaths meaningful to ourselves, we are experiencing it in symbol, in magic identification, while we are still sentient.

We are like them who have seen a great comet, yea, a great star, flash across the skies. While it cut its great saffron arc we had little to say, really. Most of us were speechless. Because our thoughts hadn't, couldn't, form, much less rise.

But now the star is gone. And even as the vapor trails are fading from view, vanishing, and its ashes are still warm at our feet, we turn to each other in amazement and begin to speak of the wondrous passing thing, and each of us brings forward his little comment, his little observation of what he thinks he saw.

Some will belittle what they saw. They will compare themselves with what he was and they will see their own shortcomings and they will seek to deny such shortcomings. Some will indulge in excessive eulogy, and forget that the real Red Lewis was mortal and human and as full of error and sin as any man. They will erase the error and fill in so as to make it seem that the whole was errorless — as was done in the case of Dickens and Hawthorne, and many another.

And some will try to forget that he ever lived. Many of them will speak out of hate, or, perhaps, only out of deep hurt. And, perhaps, that is to be expected. Afterall, when you light a hot fire there is always someone who will complain of the warmth. And even someone who will complain of having been burnt because he happened to stand too close. But, ah! for those of us who stood afar off, we speak of the light we saw and how it helped us.

Why did Red Lewis write as he did? Why couldn't he have written more sweetly, more comfortingly? Why? The psychiatrist or the analyst may perhaps tell you that it was some unresolved hurt or some unsatisfied hunger suffered in youth, yea, even in babyhood before the time of remembered consciousness, some lack that festered long enough to have invested his whole personality, which harried and drove him to get psychic justice. The man of God may perhaps say that it was some hidden or inward or deep sense of guilt or sin in his conscience that drove him on. And so on. The critic, the social worker, the lawyer, the doctor, the politician, the relative, the friend, all will have their particular theories. And, in a sense, all may be right.

For myself, since I am a simple man, I have only a simple opinion. I like to think that he wrote what he did because somewhere sometime there leaped into focus in Red two simultaneous visions, or knowledges, or insights: one, of the way things ought to be; two, of the way things were. Red Lewis was an honest man. And a man who loved justice. Thus when he saw the vast, the awful, gulf that lay between the two knowledges, he was outraged, and a fire started in him that never went out, that harried him until he gave in to it and he had to take up pen and paper.

Where these knowledges come from I can't say. Nor to my knowledge and to my satisfaction (and I have attentively searched both the blood in my veins and the ink on pages, both my heart and the scriptures) has any one else been able to explain their origins. So far all we know is that they are there and that a few of us have them consciously enough to exercise ourselves about it. Perhaps, maybe, possibly, we may someday know the mystery of the origin of these knowledges.

It is these knowledges that cause men to take up medicine, the ministry, law, artistry, social work, palmistry, to take up all those many and varied missions which cause us to say of one: he has heard The Call.

Red heard The Call too. Not to preach, or to admonish in particular, or to hurl unctuous maxims and hellfire anathemas at us. But The Call to lift a light, a lamp, so that the rest of us could clear away the lies, the deceit, the sloth, the sins of omission and of commission that beset us as humans. And not only that. But also to lift the light so that we could see what it meant to be human. Red wanted us to be active. Red believed that in action there was humanity. Red held up a flame to illuminate our way a little distance at the same time that he goaded us, even seared some of us, into action. Until we saw.

This is the charge then: do not, while you are admiring the vapor trails fading in the firmament, while you are lamenting these his ashes still warm at our feet, do not forget that Red Lewis was human and mortal and errorful; do not forget that lights eventually burn out; do not forget that someone must leap forward to grab up the torch or else much that was human shall have been lost to darkness. And do not forget that anyone of you, and all of you, are candidate torchbearers.

January 27, 1951
At Wrâlda

West of the Mississippi
An Interview with Frederick Manfred*

MR. MANFRED, WOULD YOU TELL US SOMETHING about your introduction to the writers of this area?

A: My first real contact with any Midwest writer was some time during college. I was home in the summer on vacation and had just enough English in college to feel very depressed about my background. Having heard the English prof, two profs there, exalt the Lake country and all the walks and paths there and all of Hardy's Wessex and so on, I began to feel those men were very lucky — they had a great country to write about, whereas what I had was nothing. I felt quite depressed because even at that time I had already made up my mind that I was going, some time, to be a writer. It happened that we had a doctor who loaned me books in the summertime. He had the complete set of Jack London and I had the complete works of Shakespeare. Well, I finished the Jack London that summer and asked him for more books, and he gave me a book by Rölvaag. I had never heard of him; I hadn't even heard of him in college. That was *Giants in the Earth*. I got into it about fifty or sixty pages when suddenly to my great astonishment I saw that Per Hansa's trek might have gone across the very farm I was

* By the editors of *Critique: Studies in Modern Fiction* (Winter, 1959).

sitting on, probably went over the very house I was sitting in, and went west to Split Rock Creek, and it dawned on me that this was famous country, that it was classic country because it had been written about.

Q: This was where, specifically?

A: This was in northwest Iowa. I was sitting in my father's home in Doon, Iowa. That was the first key, the first opening door in my mind, that it wasn't all lost, that my past wasn't for nothing. I think that's one of the things that I ran into as a teacher at Macalester, that these poor kids had the feeling they were to cut off everything they had been up to the time they came to college and adopt a new life, a new past, because everything they read about or were given first came from other countries—England, France, Italy, Greece, and so on — and that they weren't given enough in high school about their own writers and their own heroes. That was the first big jump in my life, and I read *Peder Victorious* and the other part of the trilogy. (That was the only book of Rölvaag I cared very much for, though — *Giants in the Earth* — and I read it once since. I think he's a good writer, but he isn't as great a writer as Lewis; he was my hero then, but he isn't any more.)

The next author I ran into was in sociology in college. This was much later, in my senior year, I think it was. I wasn't taking a course in sociology, but my best friend was, and he talked to me about his course a lot and kept mentioning Veblen. And one day I heard that Veblen was from the Northfield area. I dug into *The Theory of the Leisure Class* and I had a terrible time with it. But I liked all of it, the feel of it and the mood of it: he wrote like an old saga writer, and he reminded me a lot — his air and his manner — of my uncles, my great-uncles, who spoke Frisian, and of their stories about the Frisian past, about the time in the old country.

The next step was Lewis. Someone told me I should read *Elmer*

Gantry; I read it and I liked it very much. I enjoyed that book probably most of his. Later on when I got to read *Arrowsmith* and *Main Street* I saw that they were greater books, but while I can see where other people think Lewis is a great writer, he never really awakened my harp. (I often think of human beings as being like the harp in a piano.) Somehow the keys that Lewis played in his novels didn't waken any echoes in my harp — not too many, just a few of them here and there. We were different kinds of people, as I mentioned earlier; I always had the feeling he was kind of like a tomcat while I was more, say, in the dog or the bear field. Lewis had a fierce yellow mind that leaped. He was just in a different category.

The next contact with a Western writer was reading Herbert Krause's novel *Wind Without Rain*, which I thought was quite a good evocation of the West. Because of reading that book I got acquainted with Herb Krause. I've read all his books since. I think he's doing some interesting work about the West, and I feel somewhat of a kinship with him in the sense of trying to preserve the first attempt to establish the nuclei of a civilization out here.

Q: You're going from the Midwest to the West now, is that right?

A: He's still Midwest. Herb Krause is still Midwest. I got to know him and like him, and we get along quite well, but we're different again, quite different people. The only thing we have in common is this attempt to put down the sort of single experience which separate families had in the Midwest and in their first attempt to begin a society. I was interested in that too. Later on I ran into Stegner's books, and I liked *Big Rock Candy Mountain* very, very much. It was a tremendously moving book to me, and I felt that here was somebody who, like me, wanted to get down the arch of a life as lived in the *whole* West, not just the Midwest but the idea of living west of the Mississippi River.

My Pier in *This Is the Year* — there is almost a whole arch there in his life, the big strong man with great potential but who had a fatal weakness, an Achilles' heel — he had basically the brains but he did not yet have a trained mind to handle his environment. The culture wasn't old enough yet to tell him how to use his talent. I have one man in *This Is the Year* (the dreamer, I call him Peterson the dreamer) who tells Pier to practice soil conservation, and I use him as a kind of a voice of the new age. Not that I was particularly interested in soil conservation as such — Peterson's is just a new voice coming on, but Pier wouldn't hear this voice (Stegner's hero Bo Mason had the same problem). He heard advice in the air around him, coming at him a little bit, but he just didn't have enough background built up as a member of a flourishing society to hear it so it would nick in, would stay in.

Then I ran across Guthrie's book, *The Big Sky*. I can see why other people like his books; I think they're very good and I like to read them, but somehow I don't feel akin to him as I do to Stegner or Krause or any of the other ones. I feel much closer to Wright Morris, who describes people who have lived just long enough to have the first regret about having lived in the West. Say like married couples who by the third or fourth or sixth year finally see everything as it really is, and then there's a little period where they both think about getting a divorce, but most of the time they don't; they go on living and then they discover new values behind, which are richer than the first ones they ever thought of. And Wright Morris is in the middle of that section. He's busy showing disillusionment in most of his books but also giving hints that there is some real stuff coming up behind that. I felt a real kinship there. I won't say it was close — I feel like he's — like in the old days, when you saw a neighbor's smoke, he was already too close, twenty miles off. Not that I want to move off, or Wright Morris wants to move off, but I

can see his smoke, say, ten miles off at work, and I think I know
what he's doing over there. That's about as close as I feel to him. I
like him very much too.

Q. Why, particularly?

A: In his case? Well, for one thing, I like the style, because it
comes out of Nebraska just as Mark Twain's style came out of his
life. Henry James has a style which comes out of Boston and England. And ·Mark Twain has his style which mostly comes out of
the West, and which much later on, as Cowley and these people
have been telling us, Hemingway has followed and Faulkner has
followed. It's an idiom that comes out of the West. And they use
this as a base, as a web or matrix, of their style and their way of pre-
senting their feelings and so on, and I like that part of it. I think too
I like the people he describes because I'm acquainted with them.

Q: Do you feel that you belong to a kind of a group of Midwestern or Western writers?

A: Well, I have to say that at first I felt I was working pretty
much alone. As far as, say, Stegner or Wright Morris or Guthrie or
any of those were concerned, it wasn't until the last two or three
years that I began to feel that perhaps they were working near me.
There was no close relationship such as the Fugitive group had —
they all knew each other and inspired each other and so on — we
were too far apart ever to meet. I had one letter from Stegner; I
never had any correspondence from either Guthrie or Morris. There
has never been any direct communication.

Q: Do you think that you do not like Guthrie's work as much
or are not so much in sympathy with his work because even when
you write about the same subjects you treat them differently — what
you seek to do is somewhat different from what Guthrie seeks to do?

A: I might say that the reason I wrote *Lord Grizzly* and since
then *Riders of Judgment* and am now at work on a new one, which

you might say are Western books (people are beginning to call them Western books; I'm stuck with that; I myself didn't want to call them that) — my reason for writing them was primarily that I began to feel a thinness in my own heroes. No matter how hard I worked, how much I thought about them, somehow they did not have all the dimensions for me. They lacked something; they lacked a — what's the expression the critics throw around? — a "usable past" within themselves; there wasn't enough history or country or culture for me to throw it up to use as a background, for me to throw my characters against, to deepen them in *that* sense. Some of the novels that we think are great take on an added greatness because we're acquainted with the culture from which they come, so that the least little gesture of the author or the hero inside that book instantly evokes part of the whole background, and, if that background isn't there and the author is busy pushing the front part of the book with not much background, there's always an empty hole. So I went out — I was interested then to find the heroes or the ancestors of my men like Pier and Maury, Elof and Eric. I thought, well, maybe I should look a little more to find, not just who were their fathers and mothers, but who the people were before them on the land — fur trappers, the first mountain men, and so on. Perhaps these people left some residue in the air, not only left their marks on the soil but left them in the air and the way they handled the new thing they first hit, which transmitted itself down, say, to my grandfather and so on. And it happened that when I was doing *This Is the Year* I ran across a reference to Hugh Glass in the *South Dakota* guide book and it instantly caught my eye — this man fighting the bear alone — it struck me that here was the first real contact of the white man with the raw West. This typified it; this was the first bumping into it. And since then there has been a series of generations; they don't necessarily follow one another directly, say, in a family, but in sequence they are sitting behind these, and even further back behind the first fur trappers are the Indians who really lived here first.

Once I had that in mind, then I decided that some day I was going to write about Hugh Glass. But I didn't know how to end the story. Hugh Glass, according to history, is supposed to have forgiven the men who deserted him, and I couldn't. I could see intellectually why he'd forgive them, but I could not feel it emotionally. I had to go into his mind, into his kind of psychology, to see why he should do it, and it took me ten years before I ran into something in my own experience—something about which I became terribly enraged and had to overcome my rage and look at it dispassionately to see that it was just. I finally had the personal experience before I could find out the end of that book, *Lord Grizzly*. Then I got right at it. By that time Siouxland had come to me — the concept of Siouxland came to me when I was writing *This Is the Year* — that that would be my core, my center, from which all other novels would gradually work out because I knew that country and the people best and that somewhere in every book there would be someone related to Siouxland or someone who would live in Siouxland. And then I decided that some day I would write a series of books (like a painter who wants to fill a hall with murals, one after the other) so that when I got through I'd have something all the way from 1800 on to the day I die. *Lord Grizzly* fit part of that pattern, and that helped me make up my mind to do it. That's a different reason from Guthrie's, I think.

Q: You conceive then that this becomes a part of a saga-like pattern?

A: The whole thing. Say, like Balzac's *Human Comedy*; he tried to do all four aspects of French society — the city and the peasants and the workers and — what was the other? Mine was mostly that I wanted to get everything that I could get—a sampling of various decades from 1800 on. And I felt too that if I did three or four in the back there, then when I went back to some modern problems that I wanted to do later on, that that would help me write a better book. I have two or three ideas I've saved all this time that I hadn't been able to do because I didn't know how to handle them. They're great stories, far better stories than any I've done so far, but I did not know how to handle them or how to do them justice. I thought I had to know more about them in the past, and that's why I went after it.

Q: Now there are a couple of things I'm not clear about. You've admitted that *Lord Grizzly* can be classified as a Western book, and I gather from what you've said that you believe there is more validity to the Western tradition than the Midwestern in literature and that this is what caused you to go back to the past, the mountain men and fur trappers; and yet, on the other hand, you've spoken of Siouxland as a kind of center from which all the rest of the novels radiate?

A: Yes. Well, Hugh Glass and those men did work through Siouxland. If you widen Siouxland, if you make Siouxland a little larger, it includes Fort Kiowa where most of this took place; it's on the western outskirts of Siouxland. When I was very young, I used to sit on Saturday afternoon in front of the billiard hall and hear these old men talk about the days when they used to trap in South Dakota in the spring and in the fall — in the winters and summers they'd come back home — and they used to speak of the old trappers beyond who'd taught them the tricks — where the beaver were, where the mink were. So in my mind that was always related: Hugh Glass was part of my experience — that those men who became fur trappers and so on left the outposts of the advancing civilization, went over there, and then came back periodically to the Midwest, but they became heroes of the West. To me, somehow, Pier and Hugh Glass are somewhat similar men except that one lived at a time when there were no farms — not many farms around, and when Pier lived he had to fight his bear in the land.

Q: What was West then is now Midwest.

A: Yes, the line keeps moving further back.

Q: You speak then of the West in terms of frontier, the westering movement?

A: Yes.

Q: Do you believe then, so far as literary traditions are concerned, that the Midwest and the West have different traditions?

A: I've tried to put them together. I understand that Mr. Webb, who wrote a book called *The Great Plains*, tries to separate them. He says that there is a distinct literature that you can call "tall grass" and another that you can call "short grass" or high plains literature. The "tall grass" man is the sodder, the sod-buster, the one that built the farm. He likes to go out in the field and stick his hand in the soil and lift it up and love it and smell it and to him that's everything. The high plains boy sits on a horse and rides over it, doesn't want to touch it at all. His attitude is something like the Indian's. He [Webb] divides them up, but I think they are all part of a larger sense of the white man taming this country and each section you tame differently.

Q: Well, granted you have tried to put the traditions together for yourself, do you believe that for others the two traditions are distinct?

A: I think they are for Guthrie.

Q: Do you think that people like Walter Van Tilburg Clark and Wright Morris are writing in the same tradition?

A: No, I think those two are apart. Wright Morris is writing about the tall grass country and its breaking up, somewhat the disillusioning process, whereas Clark is quite distinctly writing (certainly in *The Ox-Bow Incident* and *The Track of the Cat*) about the Far West, the great untillable soil. The difference between tilling and non-tilling, I think there's a great difference there. You'd have some trouble putting them together.

Q: Well, in the early period, say, when there's actually Lord Grizzly fighting the bear and similarly fighting with the land, the struggle would take different forms, perhaps, but it would be the same struggle, the Western struggle?

A: Yes.

Q: But by now — would you feel that somehow during the period between the present and the struggling period there was a change in the characteristics so that, on the one hand, you get Sinclair Lewis writing about small towns and farmland, things like that; on the other hand, you have, say, Willa Cather writing about the tremendous sweep, the desert, the arid places, and the Mexican tradition?

A: She sort of puts them together, doesn't she? There's a definite influence from the Southwest moving into her work; the wind is southwest in her books, west and southwest. For Lewis, there wasn't any wind: there was a pull to get away and then to look back and to pick it apart. Cather really loved it and was full of longing for it even though she didn't live there much afterwards. I think in her novels the West and Midwest come together somewhat as in mine; I think she liked it all. I know Red Cloud quite well because part of the new book I'm writing takes place there, curiously enough — the last half of it takes place out there. It's still tillable country — it's tall grass country. But Cather also writes about the Southwest, Mexico; there is a Western atmosphere in her books.

Q: Of course, part of that difference might be attributable to Lewis' temperament as a satirist.

A: Yes. A poet tends to fix his feelings and his imagination to a certain country and to exalt it, even when sometimes he's a little rough on it. Lewis speared it and cut it. In a way he always claimed he loved it too, but he didn't operate the way that Cather did; he was a satirist.

Q: Well, you've spoken now of some of the influences on you as a writer, particularly about some of the writers that you came across as you were beginning your career. What about Walter Van Tilburg Clark?

A: I read Clark quite a few years ago. *The Ox-Bow Incident*, I think, helped me go after *Lord Grizzly*. Knowing that he had done it, I had the feeling that then I could do it too. In fact, I got more out of that book than I did out of Guthrie's; the general tone and attack appealed to me. This is what I felt about Clark: he tried to find in the flow of life a knot or a problem that would catch up a particular feeling, a particular web of life that those men lived in those days. They had to set up their own society. Some rudimentary sense of justice came along with them out there, but here they had this trouble, and what were they going to do about it? He tried to pin down the first formations of society out there, just as I tried to do in *Lord Grizzly*. He was interested in justice — it's a key to his book — and I was interested in justice in *Lord Grizzly*. I didn't read the book at the time I did *Lord Grizzly*; I made a point of staying away from it because I unfortunately am one of these people who, if I read someone, finds he moves in on me.

Q: What do you think of Vardis Fisher?

A: I didn't read Vardis Fisher early in my life and so he could never have the impact on me that he would have had if I'd read him earlier. But I've read him in the last ten years, and I like much of what he does. *The Mothers*, I thought, was a marvelous novel, very fine. It's about the Donner party going through the Sierra

Nevadas. A real fine study of the many kinds of things that I'm interested in: of people having suddenly a sort of moving community coming out of the East and having to go into a narrow pass and suddenly having to face nature for a while, and then later on having to face their own souls, their own internal natures — some of them are cannibals and some are not — and what finally saves them. It's a very fundamental study of what makes up a human being. The new book, *Tale of Valor*, is as fine a recasting as you could possibly do in the field, in the novel of well-documented historical event. It wrote itself through him more than he took it over and wrote it, but that's something he couldn't help. It's just a tremendous theme, epic in its own right; he couldn't tamper very much with it. But he did fill it out. Fisher is interesting. He first wrote about the people he knew and then took up themes further away from home; you might almost call them Western books, Western novels. That didn't quite satisfy him; he wanted to probe even deeper, so then he began this long Testament of Man series in which he went all the way back into primitive times, in Indo-Europe, and has followed that all the way out into the time of Christ. And we're now about to get into modern times, so he's going to take it into America. He's been restless as a writer out there in Idaho, and he's been somewhat unhappy with what he's found. Not only is he unhappy with the people he found, he's been somewhat unhappy with the themes he's had to deal with, so he's gone further back, beyond America, into and beyond even European civilization and the roots of European civilization — he's jumped all the way back.

Q: May I interject one other name? What about Frank Norris? Did you ever read him, or has he had any influence on you?

A: I've read *The Pit* and the one before that, *The Octopus*, there's another. You know, the style of those books never appealed to me. It didn't hit me. I read those with great interest, and I was intrigued by the idea, by the largeness of the concept, but somehow the style didn't catch me. And I never pursued them; I never went on.

Q: We've been looking at the end of *The Golden Bowl*, and in the italicized section at the end there is the same kind of celebration of the new life coming up again that you find when Norris is hitting his stride.

A: I don't remember that at all. But of course it might have caught in; I don't know. I might tell you how the ending of *The Golden Bowl* came about. I didn't know how to end that book. I didn't want to leave it in total defeat. At the same time I was working toward the center of the cyclone, not only in the book, but in a cyclone of living on the plain. Of course, living here, I'm very intrigued by the weather, tornadoes and cyclone systems, and so on, and I had in mind somewhat the device of a cyclone for the book. It never came off completely, except in the last chapter where it comes in again. And it occurred to me that I had stopped exactly in the eye of the cyclone; this was a good time for a pause and also a good time to end the book. In the center of the cyclone there is calm, and in a calm moment after a lot of commotion, people have a tendency either to let their spirits go down or to soar, and mine, mine soar. That occurred to me, and then I said, now I know how to end it. I wrote it in about a half hour. To me it's perfect; I wouldn't want anything else. That symbol came up out of the country.

Could I go on about using materials out of my area for the structure of my books? I think that's pertinent to the inquiry here. *This Is the Year* — the version that was finally published was actually the third version; the other two versions I destroyed except for four chapters I still have here in my files. The only thing I kept was the terrain, but I destroyed the people, everything — started fresh each time. The third time, I decided that my problem was the plot: what kind of a plot was I going to use? One of the twenty-six conventional plots or one out of the *Decameron* or should I try to work out a plot of my own out of my own country as Rölvaag sort of haphazardly did? I was studying weather bureau records one day when I noticed — I made a graph of them — when I noticed five interesting different swings in weather cycles, and I thought why not use this interesting weaving of the ups and downs of the particular year. I'll take one year up and one year down, one year up and two down — because I was going to make it a tragedy, of course. I found these years quite easily; they happened to fit the most dramatic years that I remember my uncles' and my father's living. And so I fitted that all over the top, and then I decided that the words, as much as I possibly could, and the actions and the height of the man as opposed to the flat lands and the stiff upright buildings, the trees and so on — that would all help build up this concept I had, first, of time flowing over a vast expanse. Whenever I found myself using a technique out of Hardy or someone else, I would quite consciously throw it away and make a sheer guess into the next chapter so that it would be as if it came right up out of the ground. This was my concept: the flowing seasons over the soil, rolling on almost like a cycle again. I've tried to do that consciously with every book since. I read everybody — Conrad, Thackeray, Smollett, all of them, Dickens, Irving — and when I'm all done I turn my back on them as much as I possibly can and try to find things in my own life or my own way of doing things, the way I might garden or the way I might, say, live with my wife or the way I get along with my relatives. I use that as a web or a line of going; I put it in my books. My feeling is that it's very difficult to be original, it's very difficult to add your little bit to the ant heap, but the more you try to be on your own, totally so, the more you might finally contribute one little bit of grain to the pile. But I think that that is an expression of Western America too: I find that amongst cowboys and lonely trappers and lonely sheepherders and lonely farmers and, incidentally, in Cather and in Lewis. Lewis had that sense too of being a definite "apart" fellow. Apartness — I think you find it in Clark and in Krause too. I think that comes up out of this Midwestern region; you don't care to know your neighbor, the writer, too much.

Q: This seems to me what you've been saying right along — that these people have not given you anything you want to imitate but you like the kind of thinking that they're doing and in your own way you do the same sort of thinking. You admire the same things they admire.

A: Yes, and I like them being lonesome. I don't mind being lonesome myself; I enjoy being lonesome. I like the old sense that my father had, and my grandfather had, of the family as a unit, of being very close; yet at the same time, how I enjoy getting into my car alone and going out West, to drive out away from town and to have experiences for myself. I enjoy them thoroughly without telling anybody about them, having a good time with it all, reading a good book alone, having a good time with the author so that I meet him in the book almost on his own ground. I enjoy that tremendously. I enjoy both things: I like people and, on the other hand, I like being alone. And I like people who like being alone. I like lonesomeness.

Q: That's different from loneliness.

A: Yes, much. Much so.

Q: One of the reasons we've asked you about some of these contemporary writers like Stegner, Clark, and so forth is to get your reaction to other writers. You've said that you think people like Clark have influenced you. Some others have not. Can you think of any other writers you especially like?

A: No, but I think if you're making a real inquiry about writers who "worked" on me or had some influence on me, I think we should not overlook three people, or things: the Bible and Shakespeare and Chaucer. The Bible had a great influence on me because it fell upon me to read the Bible at the table. So I read the Bible seven times through before I was seventeen, and knew it backwards and forwards, loved a lot of it, and read it in between times because I liked reading about the battles and I liked Job and I liked some of the prophets and some of the psalms. When I got to be sixteen or seventeen, I began to read the Song of Solomon over and over again. Wonderful thing for me.

When I was sixteen years old — between high school and college I stayed home two years — I bought a complete set of Shakespeare which I still have. I read them through on the farm while working. When I hitchhiked I took the Bible and Shakespeare and Walt Whitman with me; those three travelled with me everywhere in the suitcase, and they're battered and they're full of road dust from every state in the Union (except the South where I didn't go — I was afraid of the chain gangs, so I didn't go to the South; I'm sorry I didn't now). The old Bible I got when I got through grade school, the Shakespeare I got in high school, and the *Leaves of Grass* I bought just as I graduated from college.

I mentioned Chaucer; I didn't know much about Chaucer until college, and there I had a course in English where the professor read a little Chaucer for us. And as he read, it hit me suddenly that the sound of this language was similar to the Frisian that my uncles spoke. That was the first time that it dawned on me that being a Frisian was an honorable thing. You see, I grew up in a community where there were New Englanders; they were the ones who settled Doon, Iowa. They controlled the community. Later on the Dutch moved in, or the Hollanders; among the Hollanders were Frisians.

The Dutchmen let you know quite soon that to be Frisian was something to be looked down upon, because in Friesland, back home in
Holland at least, they were boers or sailors, and they never got
beyond that. (I might add quickly here that my father was a West
Frisian from Holland.) So I went out into life thinking, first, I was
a minority amongst Hollanders and, then, Hollanders were a minority amongst Americans, and I had to punch up through two layers
to get out to where there were Americans, when all along my father
already felt like an American and talked like it. Yet when I went
into life I always had a sort of a double inhibition to break through.
But in college I first heard that the Frisian language was really Old
English. To my great joy, I then started going into it further and
further, and when I lived at the University, Red Warren helped
me — suggested a few books I should get if I was interested in it —
Chaucer. I now have an old set of Chaucer which is as worked over
as the Bible, and those four [the Bible, Chaucer, Shakespeare, and
Whitman] really had as much to do with my life as Lewis and
Cather and some of the other ones have — probably more. They
were probably the entering spear of culture from the East into me.

Q: Did reading Chaucer and Shakespeare give you a sense of
being soaked in an English as well as an American literary tradition?

A: No. For one thing, Shakespeare writes about Julius Caesar
and Hamlet, subject matter that isn't always English and except for
having, say, a longing to see Stratford-on-Avon, I don't think it
worked on me particularly that he was English — just that he was
a very great writer and also that he used strong racy language. At
times this appealed to me as a man from the West, so that, for example, I wouldn't care at all for Ben Jonson, but I would like Shakespeare very much. As a Western man, I like those direct expressions.
The same thing with Chaucer. The thing that Chaucer did for me
was to sort of help me throw off that yoke of being called a Hol-

lander and a Dutchman which I had in the name of Feikema. I'd never felt like a Dutchman; my family very strictly taught us that we were not Hollanders. We were Frisians if anything, but Grandpa loved being an American — could speak the language very well; he had little difficulty learning it because in the Frisian language the basic words are very similar to the English words. For "through" they say *troch*; for "stone" they say *stein*; for "cheese" they say *tsiis*. So Grandpa taught us early that we were American; yet people were calling us Hollanders. That always disturbed me. Chaucer helped me get rid of that sense of particular race or ethnic group by discovering, well, if it came down to it, I was actually as English as you could possibly get, and I still loved being a Western American.

Q: Now we move on to a couple of other things. Are you in communication with any of your contemporary American writers?

A: No, none of them, as far as I can think. I've met many writers off and on, more or less, at one time or another, but I don't correspond much with any of them. I have corresponded with — I have to think about that. That answers your question right there: I have to think and scratch my mind.* I have written and do correspond occasionally with Van Wyck Brooks. I've had letters from him — a dozen or so over a period of ten years — in which he has scolded me for not soaking up and sort of investing my plot or relating my plot with the environment and filling it in and tying it in with the

---

* Actually, I have corresponded, off and on, occasionally, with: William Carlos Williams, Robert Penn Warren, Nelson Algren, J. F. Powers, Alan Swallow, Vardis Fisher, John R. Milton, Herbert Krause, Jack Conroy, Peter DeVries, David Cornel Delong, Russell Roth, Henry Miller, John Dos Passos, Fred Babcock, Emmett Dedmon, Sinclair Lewis, Bernard DeVoto, Dan Brennan, Ray West, Malcolm Cowley, Meindert DeJong, Ray Smith, William Van O'Connor. Part of my reluctance to mention this correspondence is due to my distaste for name-dropping. Somehow it is bad taste to mention such correspondence. Such matters are personal.

sense of the rest of the country. But you see I can't do that. Mr. Van Wyck Brooks lives in New England, a much older section, and he feels part of it and part of its history. We're still busy building it out here. It is difficult for me to feel as tied to what I'm supposed to be tied to as he is to what he's got.

Q: It's really because you wanted some usable past, as you mentioned, that you wanted to do things like *Lord Grizzly*? You don't sense any presentness of the past — in the Midwest especially?

A: Every mile I go west, I do. When I take a trip out, the further west I go, the more I feel that those people remember the old days more than they do, say, in the town of Minneapolis. I think the town of Minneapolis looks east and looks to Paris and New York on almost every scale, and to Europe more and more as the years go by. They have centennials and they try to remind you of the old days and so on, but I think that's mostly water off a duck's back in the larger towns here. But in the smaller towns and in the open country, I think they do remember the past.

Q: That's what you find attractive in Walter Van Tilburg Clark's work?

A: Yes, and that's what I find attractive in leaving town and driving west, why I like to go back to my home, which is just a short ways away from here, and visit. I want it to be a great place, and therefore I look for heroes in it and I try to celebrate them.

Q: This may overlap somewhat with some of the other questions, but we'd like to ask you again about the matter of ethnic groups. You've already talked some about the Frisians.

A: Well, you know in the beginning many little towns had them. Say New Ulm would be solid German; Orange City, Iowa, would be mostly Dutch; Holdingford would be Norwegian; Askov, Minnesota, would be Danish; Floodwood would be Finnish — in the beginning when they were first settled. As time goes on, though, a great intermarriage has been going on continually; that has intrigued me about Siouxland because you'll have these little spotted centers over Siouxland which were originally separated but now they're pretty much intermarried, and I notice that. I get the three weeklies from down there, and I watch the marriages, and I notice a great intermingling of peoples. Now, when I wrote *This Is the Year* I didn't mean particularly to celebrate the Frisians as Frisians; it just happened that I knew something about them, and I thought it would be intriguing to describe such a small embryo settlement which never really will take hold. Eventually it will break up, as it did, and as is happening now. That is part of my reason for it, but I could as well have written about the Norwegians or any other one. I didn't particularly mean to celebrate any one group. I wanted to show that eventually they do intermarry. Even Pier the hero. He marries a Norwegian girl from the north a ways. And the legends that his father had disappear — pieces of them remain, and they're transformed and taken over much the way that the Christians took the pagan beliefs in the old days and adopted them into the Christian religion. So, too, I think that the general American stamp will eventually make these people a homogeneous group. It's continually going on.

Q: I believe in *The Primitive* you speak of the ethnic groups coming and taking over the tradition of the New Englanders who first settled. Do you believe this is all part of the melting process?

A: Yes. They're all fitting into the mold. The New Englanders set it; they put the town hall in, the constables, and the relationship of the township to the county and so on; and these other people come in and they fill that set. For a little while they hold on to their religions, their little private house gods, and the way they run their weddings. Going back to your observation about the difference between books about the Midwest and the Far West, what I meant to do a little bit in *Riders of Judgment* was to pull the two together, in my mind anyway. I took people—or the feel of people that I have— that I know back home in Siouxland, and I put them in Wyoming. The models for the heroes came out of Siouxland, and I had an intention for that in this sense, that people, if they're unhappy in Siouxland, if they're a little on the roisterous side or the community is a little too tight for them or close, where people are living as too close neighbors, then . . . .

Q: Is Siouxland a way of designating a geographical location and of suggesting an intense Midwesternness, or do you feel the peculiar Indianness in the background somehow? This occurs to me because I know that someone like Walter Van Tilburg Clark has been quite explicit about his feelings toward the Indians — someone like Joe Sam in *The Track of the Cat.* Clark said once he had come increasingly to feel that the most important man on the North American continent was the Indian.

A: Well, I'd almost say that even today. I use the word "Siouxland" definitely because the Sioux lived there. My grandfather told me that when he first came here he ran into the Sioux, and one of my relatives, some three or four generations back, when they came in their wagons, rather late in the summer, knew it was too late to plant any corn or wheat, yet wondered if he couldn't get in some garden produce like, say, radishes or lettuce. When he talked about this, an Indian overheard him—a man named Yellowsmoke—and showed him where to go to plant. They didn't have a plow and the sod was too tough to break up with a spade. So he told him to go to these mounds that the pocket gophers made and to sow their radish seeds and lettuce there. And I remember very vividly, when they told me that as a boy, that really put the Indian right into my mind.

Then as part of my process, which I talked about earlier, of going back to find heroes, or pre-heroes, or early-day heroes to my modern-day heroes, I discovered in studying Hugh Glass that he was in many ways part Indian himself. In fact, of course, the fur trappers and mountain men lived with the Indians and married 'em and got along very well with the Indians. There wasn't any argument there. The argument came later on when the traders, that is, the merchant men, came in and the missionaries came in; then with the ledgerman and the storekeeper, that's when the trouble set in, but in the early days the Indian got along very well with the white man. Hugh Glass had some Indian in him, and behaved somewhat like an Indian, lived like an Indian; well, then I knew that some day I'd have to go back before his time to write a book about that. That occurred about fifteen-twenty years ago in my mind, and I began to collect things in my memory and also in my notebooks about some possible book about Indians and about my country, Siouxland — a book which I'm now writing. It's a book about the Yankton Sioux before the white man reached them.

Q: Well, how does this all fit in with the other ethnic groups that figure in your work, which are all openly of European stock?

A: Well, for one thing, the Indian is related to, closely and warmly related to, the soil of this country; he was part of the ecology and got along with it and was doing fine and I think was slowly evolving up the ladder of becoming civilized. He was many years behind the ladder in Europe, which had begun earlier; but he was moving up on his own speed here, probably about as fast. Suddenly we broke in on that and disrupted it completely, and for a little while we had to contend with him as well as the environment. After we have dispersed him — we think — we discover we too have come to terms with the same environment that he came to terms with — only, we have different tools. We discover that if we're not careful with the land it runs away on us, erodes away or is washed away. We're just now learning a little bit about how to build a house that is warm in the winter and as snug and comfortable as his was, the tepee in his days. Then, maybe I'm a little bit of a mystic here, but what brings them together in my mind is that you're continually running into the ghosts of the old boys around here. It's as if this land has its own souls and it evolves its own souls — the Indian has his particular soul and now the white man has come in and he has to forget the soul he has and — this is treacherous ground, by the way. I realize it. I'm not a philosopher and I'm not a professional psychologist, but I nevertheless still feel very strongly that there is something going on in the relationship of the human being to his environment. Eventually it makes his soul. I think you're given the nervous equipment to have a soul; that's all you're given at birth. After that your environment makes you whatever you are, makes your soul. And I think that we're beginning to have our own original soul out here. And I find in my mind some conflict whenever I listen too sharply to Chaucer or too sharply to Shakespeare — that then I lose a feeling for what I am out here, as Fred from Siouxland, and naming that country Siouxland helped sort of crystallize a lot of things in my mind. When I built this mural, I could see the first people almost; the land remained the same, but the animals keep changing as you go on. You see all the way in here, from the early things that come out of the sea and gradually some four-legged animals, then upright, and so on. The soil always remains the same, but the creatures change a little bit. The outside of the creatures may change a little bit, but the inside, I think, remains the same.

Q: This is all tied up with lonesomeness in a way, isn't it?

A: Yes.

Q: In other words, being out here is a way of identifying yourself?

A: Yes. That's exactly right, because if you get too sociable then the other stuff comes in, pours in on you, that doesn't belong here quite yet. We have to be our own kind of roughnecks in this country before we can develop our set of manners. That's the way I feel. Ransom wrote an article some time ago about the rednecks, or the roughnecks, in American letters. I thought, well, so what, the early Saxons were known as hearty beef eaters and strong ale drinkers and were ruffians of the first order, and it took them five hundred years before they developed this very high-toned Oxonian accent and set of manners. And we've got to have about the same amount of time to develop our particular set, and I think there is a distinct difference between the kind of guy that's going to develop out of the Midwest as well as the Far West in time to come, who will be a distinct fellow with a peculiar and separate way of behaving than the English gentleman, as well as, say, the French cavalier and the Spanish caballero. We aren't old enough out here to have our own set of manners.

Q: But then Siouxland for you is not only geographical, it's spiritual?

A: It's spiritual, oh, yes! Oh, yes. To me it isn't just Minnesota. It's a piece of four states, and so that sort of lifts it even geographically above just being one state. It becomes the upper part of the Mississippi valley. I have the feeling — I haven't pinned this down yet by enough reading — but I have the feeling that the writers from the northern half of the Mississippi valley and the writers of the southern half feel more as a group, more brotherly towards each other, than do, say, the writers of the Piedmont. I heard Allen Tate talk a little bit about that one night; I didn't catch all of it, but he had somewhat the same feeling. I feel a great deal of kinship to Tate and Warren and Faulkner; different as we are, they are lonesome too. And I think part of my feeling is due to the fact that all my life I've regarded the Mississippi valley as one entity. If you look at the Mississippi, it's like a tree with branches going out, and we all pour into it, even though we did come in from the East to settle it, some of us. Many of us also came up the river and gradually branched out over these rivers. As time went on, we set up civilizations in these river towns, and they were there first. I think that's part of the reason why I'm interested in Hugh Glass and in some of these other western themes, that they came in via the river, whereas some of the older people that I write about came in from the East as immigrants. But they still have to come together on these rivers and get caught in this vast interlocking web. And I think that America has in the Mississippi River a sort of Nile of Egypt. We even have some towns named alike — Memphis, and Cairo — and we have a great seaport down at the far end very similar to the seaport off the end of the Nile. The Nile periodically overflows its banks and reawakens the land over there, and our Mississippi periodically overflows. There are many similarities of the two rivers, in the way they affect the people, and I think the Nile tends to unite the people in Egypt, just as I think the Mississippi tends to unite everybody here.

Q: I noticed, is it *Morning Red*, is dedicated to Faulkner; is that part of your attempt to express that kinship?

A: Yes, it is. I like him a lot. There's much in him that appeals to me. I'd say a good half of his work is warm to me. I'm immediately in it, and it's as if a better part of me could have written it — not that I could do it, but a better part of me could have written it. The other half I don't quite get. It may be that it's due to the fact that Mississippi is warm and humid and has bayous and mosquitos and so on and is damper; the air is muggy and sort of unclear most of the day, whereas up here the air most of the time, or about half of the time, is very clear with clean, strong north Canadian winds and so on. There's a difference there, and that causes me to feel a little uneasy about half of it. Or it may be in the character of Faulkner himself as a person.

Q: Do you know him?

A: No. I've never met him. I wrote him that I was dedicating the book to him, but he didn't acknowledge it or anything. He plays possum a lot, you know. His smoke signal is almost out of sight. But there's something else that appeals to me. I haven't done too much of it — I'd like to; maybe he has more daring than I to do it. If a human mind can be considered to be, say, a four-walled room or a walled room, then Faulkner has a three-walled room with one wall open to nature — to the wilds. And you're not aware of it, by the way. You know, you're used to reading the proper Thackeray, and all these other proper writers who have conventional walls around what they are doing . . . and then you get into Faulkner's room and you sit there a little while and you're reading, and all of a sudden it dawns on you that there are some strange things going on: you look at the floor, and there's an alligator crawling right past your chair and there goes a vine lifting and crawling and moving. It's very horrifying for a little while, that this nature is just sort of breathing, pulsing, in and out of that wall that's gone, into this room, and it gives you the terrible shivers. He really lets the old dinosaurs get into his books, the old *far* past time; they get in sort of automatically in that man. And I think that helps explain some of his style once in a while, these serpentine sentences, you know.

Q: Something terribly primitive, like Stravinsky's music.

A: Yes . . . Yes . . . . It's quiet! as nature is at first. Until the jump, see, until the pounce.

July 13, 1958
At Wrâlda